RECI
&
MENUS

Michel-Ange Publishing

Translator: June Rogers
Proofreader: Veronica Schami
Cover: Serge Hudon
Layout: Luc Jacques, Compomagny
Printing: AGMV Marquis

Michel-Ange Publishing, 1999
National Library of Canada
National Library of Québec

Canadian Cataloguing in Publication Canada
Montignac, Michel
Lacombe, Isabelle
Diet Technician
Recipes & Menus

ISBN: 0-9684029-2-5

To order copies of this book, please contact the Canadian distributor, Prologue Inc. Telephone: 1-800-363-2864. Fax: (450) 434-4135.

MICHEL MONTIGNAC

RECIPES
&
MENUS

with Isabelle Lacombe,
Diet Technician

TABLE OF CONTENTS

PREFACE

The World Health Organization recently sounded the alarm: our entire planet is facing an epidemic of obesity.

For many years, we naively believed that excess weight was primarily a North American phenomenon. Slowly but surely, however, problems with weight began showing up in all industrialized countries, although they haven't reached the critical level yet.

Up until now, the thinking about obesity went like this: weight gain occurs when a person eats too much and exercises too little.

Since 1997, however, this thinking has been proven false. In the United States and elsewhere, scientific studies are beginning to shed new light on this old belief.

Consider this: Over the last 20 years, Westerners have flocked to exercise as never before. Indeed, physical exercise in all permutations and combinations has become a major phenomenon as has the consumption of fat-free foods. Still, obesity continues to rise. The phenomenon has become known as the American Paradox.

In 1986, when my first book was published (*Eat Yourself Slim*), I addressed this glaring contradiction. My explanation went like this: If North Americans were becoming more and more obese, as is the rest of the world, it was not due to excess eating. North Americans were becoming fat because of the poor quality of food they ate.

Three factors account for this phenomenon:

1. The tumultuous socioeconomic factors of modern society.
2. The industrialization of agricultural production.
3. The bad eating habits of Western societies.

All of these factors are interrelated, because each one is a result of the other.

After the Second World War, little more than 50 years ago, Western society underwent a major shift. With increased urbanization, and the abandonment of farms, Western populations became concentrated in fewer places – namely cities.

As a result, food was not grown in the same place that it was consumed. Transporting food required new methods to keep it from spoiling, namely chemical preservatives and freezing. As well, more food was needed to feed the enormous baby boom generation. As a result, a veritable revolution occurred in the way food was manufactured. Food production became more mechanized, and chemical fertilizers, pesticides and herbicides were required to make food grow more quickly and efficiently.

When women began to flow into the workforce in record numbers, food manufacturers responded by creating faster ways to cook meals for time-strapped families. More often than not, meals were served from cans, frozen packages, TV dinners and fast-food outlets. Wholesome meals prepared at home became the exception.

This transformation of our food landscape happened so quickly that no one could possibly predict its eventual harmful effects. But finally, with several decades of poor eating behind us, we have finally come to understand that this transformation in the way we eat did not come without consequences.

Due to this drastic change, we are now experiencing an increase in diseases: diabetes, cancer, multiple sclerosis, Alzheimer's, cardiovascular diseases and, of course, obesity.

With the Montignac Method, I not only correctly identified the reason for the rise in obesity, but I also proposed a solution that has endured the test of time and has been disseminated all around the world.

The Montignac Method is based on two observations:

1. The utter failure of traditional dieting methods, which state that in order to lose weight you have to eat less and exercise

more. After 20 years of this kind of thinking, studies now show that not only does traditional dieting not work, it has actually increased the rate of obesity.

2. Contrary to popular belief, studies now show that exercise does not prevent weight gain.

The real reasons for weight gain and consequent obesity are: the poor quality of overprocessed foods, which are eaten in all industrialized countries; and bad eating habits.

It is precisely the lack of nutritional value (vitamins, minerals, essential fatty acids, fibre and the molecular structure of starches) that causes weight problems. The body is unable to digest processed foods properly, which leads to an abnormal storage of fat.

Choosing foods high in nutritional value, which the Montignac Method recommends, will allow optimal digestion of foods, which in turn helps to maintain an ideal weight. Changing eating habits also produces health benefits: a decrease in cholesterol, triglycerides, diabetes, chronic fatigue syndrome, migraines and intestinal problems. The Montignac Method recommendations are, in effect, a real solution to the world's health problems.

This book reflects the principles of the Montignac Method. The recipes and menus are easy to prepare and were designed by a diet technician who is familiar with the North American diet. All of the ingredients are easy to find at your local stores, which would not be the case if the recipes were typically French.

However, a number of principles not common to North Americans have been introduced. For example, I recommend several alternatives when it comes to cooking with fats.

I highly recommend the use of olive oil in all cooking preparations, especially when there is a call for butter.

Even though butter is nutritious with its high vitamin A content, it should be eaten in moderation. Because it is a saturated fat, you should not eat more than 2 Tbsp a day. Also, you should never use it for cooking. When it is heated, butter deteriorates to such an extent that it is difficult to digest and can even become carcinogenic.

High heat can also cause other foods to lose their nutritional value. That is why I recommend that you eat foods raw or cook foods on low heat whenever possible.

As for the menus that are included in this book, please note that they are only suggestions. Each meal or day is interchangeable, as long as you choose among a variety of foods.

Cooking is as much an art as painting or composing music. That's why eating is such a pleasure. The biggest joy that we can derive from good food is to share it with our family and friends, especially after we've prepared it with care and love.

Michel Montignac

FOREWORD

SOMETHING BETTER THAN BUTTER?

When it comes to cooking, butter should be banned forever.

Granted, many cookbooks will tell you to use butter for cooking, especially the ones by renowned chefs. Even in the classic cookbooks from Provence, a number of recipes call for butter.

This practice began when butter used to be rare and expensive, and therefore valuable. Cuisine au beurre was the prerogative of the rich, first with aristocrats and then the bourgeoisie, and their chefs obliged with the creation of a number of dishes that incorporated butter. Indeed, France's gastronomical tradition was essentially founded on a base of butter.

A visit to the great restaurants of France will inevitably reveal the honoured place butter occupies. It is not uncommon to find a large vat of clarified butter sitting as on a throne in a double boiler next to the stove in the nation's best kitchens. Famous chefs will tell you that by clarifying butter at 250°F (120°C), it is reduced to its pure fat base without impurities, and its colour more closely resembles its original natural yellow. Clarified butter is used in all manner of cooking, from baking to roasting, and especially in the preparation of many sauces.

While butter is essentially a beneficial nutrient when it is eaten fresh on a piece of toast, for example, or slightly melted (in moderation, no more than 25 g/2 Tbsp a day), this is not the case when it is used in cooking. Butter is a saturated fat, composed of essential fatty acids that are easily digested. But once butter is heated over 212°F (100°C), the essential fatty acids are basically destroyed. Cooked butter becomes harmful to your health because your stomach enzymes cannot digest it properly. Once butter is heated to 250°F (120°C), it is totally altered and burns, which in turn creates acrolein, a well-known carcinogen. And when one uses butter in traditional baking recipes in which temperatures reach 320°F to 350°F (160°C to 180°C), it becomes even more noxious.

This is why I recommend goose or duck fat when cooking with temperatures higher than 212°F (100°C).

Goose or duck fat, which can be found at your local fine butcher stores, has three advantages. First, it is basically a monounsaturated fat. It has the same chemical structure as olive oil, which has been proven to be good for your health. Second, goose fat can also withstand high temperatures (in excess of 392°F/200°C) without its molecular structure being destroyed. Thus, it is easily digested as well as beneficial to cardiovascular health. Third, but not least, goose fat imbues food with a delicious taste, enhancing its gastronomical value. Goose fat. It's better than butter when it comes to cooking.

LIST OF RECIPES

SOUPS

SALADS

VINAIGRETTES & SALAD DRESSINGS

EGGS

VEGETABLE SIDE DISHES

LEGUMES & GRAINS

DESSERTS

MENUS: WEEK 1

	MONDAY	TUESDAY	WEDNESDAY	THURSDAY	FRIDAY	SATURDAY	SUNDAY
L U N C H	*Greek Salad	*Cold Cream of Asparagus Soup	Crudités in *Tangy Dip	*Cream of Cauliflower Soup	*Avocado Salad	*Lentil Soup	Tomato Salad
	*Turkey Scallops with Herbs & Sour Cream	Filet Mignon	*Salmon Steaks	Chicken with Thyme	*Veal Brochettes	Chicken Salad	*Broccoli Omelette
	Broccoli	*Ratatouille	*Crisp Vegetables with Sour Cream	Steamed Vegetables			
	*Pears Poached in Wine	Cheese	*Raspberry & Almond Delight	Cheese	Cheese	Cheese	*Raspberry Snow
D I N N E R	Leek Soup	*Rainbow Salad	Green Salad	*Alfalfa Sprout Salad	Mushroom Soup	Squash Salad	Cabbage Soup
	*Spicy Shrimp with Ginger	*Mexican Omelette	*Meal-in-One Soup	*Vegetarian Chili	*Trout Surprise	*Spicy Lasagna	Tuna Fish
	Oriental Vegetables				Green Beans	Cauliflower	Mushrooms
	Yogurt	*Frozen Berry Soufflé	**Yogurt	*Frozen Chocolate Yogurt	Unsweetened Dark Chocolate with 70% (Minimum) Cocoa	**Yogurt	Yogurt

* See recipe.
** Flavour with unsweetened fruit jam or unsweetened apple sauce.

18

MENUS: WEEK 2

	MONDAY	TUESDAY	WEDNESDAY	THURSDAY	FRIDAY	SATURDAY	SUNDAY
L U N C H	Green Salad	*Italian Garden Salad	Cream of Broccoli Soup	*Creamy Cucumber Salad	*Alfalfa Sprout Salad	*Sugar Peas & Curly Lettuce Salad	Cream of Vegetable Soup
	*Veal Chops with Chervil & Capers	*Stuffed Chicken Scallops	Egg Salad	*Chicken Croquettes	*Roast Beef with Red Wine	*Moroccan-Style Chicken	*Haddock Fillets with Almonds
	Lemon Asparagus	*Grilled Zucchini		*Red & Yellow Pepper Medley		Zucchini & Green Pepper Brochettes	*Cauliflower & Zucchini Curry
		Cheese	Cheese	Unsweetened Dark Chocolate with 70% (Min.) Cocoa	Cheese	Cheese	
	*Crème brûlée						*Lemon Sorbet
D I N N E R	*Cream of Spinach Soup	Vegetable Soup	Lettuce Salad	Crudités	Hearts of Palm	Endive Salad	Green Pepper Salad
	*Fish Fillets with Tomato Sauce & Red Peppers	*Lemon Dill Lentil & Chickpea Salad	*Turkey with Peas & Tomatoes	*Brown Basmati Rice & Black Beans	*Seafood Brochettes	*Pea Soup	Scrambled Eggs
	Mushrooms						
	Yogurt	*Chocolate Custard	Yogurt	**Yogurt	Yogurt	*Coconut Custard with Berries	Yogurt

* See recipe.

** Flavour with unsweetened fruit jam or unsweetened apple sauce.

MENUS: WEEK 3

	MONDAY	TUESDAY	WEDNESDAY	THURSDAY	FRIDAY	SATURDAY	SUNDAY
LUNCH	Watercress Soup	*Spinach & Bean Sprout Salad	*Rainbow Salad	Cream of Red Pepper Soup	*Onion Soup	*Avocado Salad	*Fish Soup
	*Meat Loaf	*Oriental Chicken Kebabs	*Red Pepper & Black Olive Frittata	*Shrimp & Hearts of Palm Salad	*Stuffed Green Peppers	*Marinated Pork Chops	*Scallop Gratin
	Green Beans					Garlic Mushrooms	
	Cheese	Cheese	*Raspberry Snow	Cheese	*Pears Poached in Wine	Cheese	Unsweetened Dark Chocolate 70% (Min.) Cocoa
DINNER	*Creamy Cucumber Salad	*Minestrone	Tomato Soup	Crudités with *Tzatziki	Green Salad	Tomato Salad	*Caesar Salad
	*Stuffed Rainbow Trout	*Bean & Chickpea Salad	*Indian-Style Chicken	*Millet & Vegetable Salad	*Salmon Tidbits	Omelette	*Mediterranean Stew
	Vegetables en Papillote		Grilled Mushrooms		*Red & Yellow Pepper Medley		
	Yogurt	**Yogurt	Yogurt	*Strawberry Mousse	Yogurt	Yogurt	**Yogurt

* See recipe.
** Flavour with unsweetened fruit jam or unsweetened apple sauce.

20

MENUS: WEEK 4

		MONDAY	TUESDAY	WEDNESDAY	THURSDAY	FRIDAY	SATURDAY	SUNDAY
L U N C H		*Spinach & Carrot Salad with Orange Dressing	*Greek Salad	Coleslaw	Crudités with *Cottage Cheese Spread	*Caesar Salad	*Sugar Peas & Curly Lettuce Salad	*Cream of Spinach Soup
		*Pork & Bean Sprouts	Grilled Turkey Breast	*Tomatoes Stuffed with Eggs	*Sole en Papillote	Filet Mignon	*Chicken Cacciatore	*Jambalaya
			Asparagus Gratin		Broccoli & Cauliflower	Mushroom & Onion Sauté	*Grilled Zucchini	
		*Raspberry Cheesecake	*English Custard	Cheese	*Raspberry Bavarian Cream	Cheese	Cheese	Cheese
D I N N E R		Cream of Broccoli Soup	Vegetable Soup	*Lentil Soup	*Spinach & Bean Sprout Salad	Crudités with *Tzatziki	*Cold Cream of Asparagus Soup	Green Salad
		Salmon Salad	Wholewheat Pasta & *Tofu Tomato Sauce	*Stuffed Chicken Scallops	*Rice & Lentils	*Broccoli Omelette	*Wild Rice Salad	Bouillabaisse
				*Ratatouille				
		Yogurt	**Yogurt	Unsweetened Dark Chocolate with 70% (Min.) Cocoa	**Yogurt	Yogurt	*Chocolate Mousse	Yogurt

* See recipe.
** Flavour with unsweetened fruit jam or unsweetened apple sauce.

21

MENUS: WEEK 5

	MONDAY	TUESDAY	WEDNESDAY	THURSDAY	FRIDAY	SATURDAY	SUNDAY
L U N C H	Cream of Mushroom Soup	*Pea Soup	Smoked Oysters	*Italian Garden Salad	*Cream of Cauliflower Soup	Cucumber & Green Pepper Salad	*Cold Cream of Asparagus Soup
	Grilled Calf's Liver	Chicken Salad	*Trout Surprise	Scrambled Eggs & Ham	*Andalusian Red Peppers & Beef	Curry Chicken	*Ginger Salmon
			Green Beans			Sautéed Vegetables	Steamed Broccoli, Cauliflower & Mushrooms
	*Crisp Vegetables with Sour Cream			Unsweetened Dark Chocolate with 70% (Min.) Cocoa			
	Chocolate Fondue	Cheese	Cheese		*Crème Brûlée	Cheese	*Coconut Mounds
D I N N E R	Green Salad	Stuffed Mushroom Caps	Tomato Salad	*Cold Cream of Asparagus Soup	*Rainbow Salad	Vegetable Soup	Cabbage Soup
	Scampi	*Three-Cheese Macaroni	*Chicken Breasts with Orange & Ginger	Tofu and Vegetable Brochettes	*John Dory with Romano Cheese	*Tabbouleh	*Mushroom Omelette Soufflé
	*Leeks in Cream		Broccoli Gratin		*Eggplant & Tomato Gratin		
	Yogurt	**Yogurt	Yogurt	Unsweetened Apple Sauce	Yogurt	*Frozen Chocolate Yogurt	Yogurt

* See recipe.
** Flavour with unsweetened fruit jam or unsweetened apple sauce.

22

MENUS: WEEK 6

	MONDAY	TUESDAY	WEDNESDAY	THURSDAY	FRIDAY	SATURDAY	SUNDAY
LUNCH	Alfalfa Sprout Salad *Stuffed Zucchini *Strawberry Mousse	Chef Salad Grilled Fish Tomatoes & Mushrooms Cheese	*Avocado Salad Egg Salad Cheese	Green Salad *Stuffed Rainbow Trout * Red & Yellow Pepper Medley Cheese	Rainbow Salad *Cajun Veal Stew Unsweetened Dark Chocolate with 70% (Min.) Cocoa	Crudités with *Tangy Dip *Moroccan-Style Chicken *Ratatouille *Glazed Apple Tart	Green Salad *Lamb & Vegetable Casserole Broccoli Cheese
DINNER	* Cream of Cauliflower Soup *Shrimp & Scallops with Leeks Yogurt	*Minestrone Soup *Vegetarian Chili *Raspberry Snow	*Cream of Spinach Soup *Turkey with Peas & Tomatoes Yogurt	Parsley Soup *Spicy Lasagna *Coconut Custard with Berries	*Pea Soup Cheese Soufflé Green Beans Yogurt	Cream of Broccoli Soup *Stuffed Eggplant **Yogurt	Cream of Celery Soup *Broiled Tuna Steaks *Green Peas & Pearl Onions Yogurt

* See recipe.
** Flavour with unsweetened fruit jam or unsweetened apple sauce.

23

MENUS: WEEK 7

	MONDAY	TUESDAY	WEDNESDAY	THURSDAY	FRIDAY	SATURDAY	SUNDAY
L U N C H	Coleslaw	*Caesar Salad	Tomato Soup	*Italian Garden Salad	Hearts of Palm	Vegetable Soup	Green Salad
	*Veal Slivers with Vegetables	*Turkey Crackling	*Haddock Fillets with Almonds	Vegetarian Omelette	*Marinated Pork Chopd	*Chicken Cacciatore	Grilled Fish
			*Cauliflower & Zucchini Curry		Green Beans	Broccoli	*Brussels Sprouts
	*Raspberry Bavarian Cream	Cheese	Cheese	Unsweetened Dark Chocolate with 70% (Min.) Cocoa	Cheese	Cheese	Cheese
D I N N E R	*Cold Cream of Asparagus Soup	*Lentil Soup	*Rainbow Salad	*Sugar Peas & Curly Lettuce Salad	Spring Greens Salad	*Creamy Cucumber Salad	*Creamy Tomato-Yogurt Soup
	Crabmeat Salad	*Red Pepper & Black Olive Frittata	*Turkey Scallops with Dijon Mustard	*Meal-in-One Soup	* Poached Fish	*Cheese & Spinach Rolls	*Pasta Salad
			*Crisp Vegetables with Sour Cream		*Red & Yellow Pepper Medley		
	Yogurt	*Frozen Berry Soufflé	Yogurt	**Yogurt	Yogurt	*Chocolate Mousse	*Lemon Sorbet

* See recipe.
** Flavour with unsweetened fruit jam or unsweetened apple sauce.

MENUS: WEEK 8

	MONDAY	TUESDAY	WEDNESDAY	THURSDAY	FRIDAY	SATURDAY	SUNDAY
L U N C H	*Italian Garden Salad	*Cream of Spinach Soup	*Avocado Salad	*Lentil Soup	Watercress Soup	*Alfalfa Sprout Salad	*Chicken Consommé with Eggs
	*Stuffed Green Peppers	*Turkey Breasts with Apricots	*Tomatoes Stuffed with Eggs	*Spicy Shrimp with Ginger	*Lamb & Vegetable Casserole	*Chicken Cacciatore	Tuna Salad
		Broccoli & Cauliflower		*Eggplant & Tomato Gratin		Green Beans	
	Cheese	Cheese	Unsweetened Dark Chocolate with 70% (Min.) Cocoa	Cheese	*Coconut Custard with Berries	Cheese	*Strawberry Mousse
D I N N E R	Tomato Juice	Lettuce Salad	Crudités with *Chickpea & Shrimp Dip	Shredded Carrot Salad	*Spinach & Bean Sprout Salad	*Cold Cream of Asparagus Soup	*Spinach & Carrot Salad with Orange Dressing
	*Stuffed Rainbow Trout	Wholewheat Pasta with *Lentil Sauce	*Oriental Chicken Kebabs	*Pea Soup	Grilled Lobster	*Mexican Omelette	*Mediterranean Stew
	*Ratatouille				*Leeks in Cream	Cucumbers & Tomatoes	
	*Crème Brûlée	**Yogurt	Yogurt	*Frozen Chocolate Yogurt	Yogurt	Unsweetened Dark Chocolate with 70% (Min.) Cocoa	Yogurt

* See recipe.
** Flavour with unsweetened fruit jam or unsweetened apple sauce.

MENUS: WEEK 9

	MONDAY	TUESDAY	WEDNESDAY	THURSDAY	FRIDAY	SATURDAY	SUNDAY
L U N C H	Artichoke Hearts	*Greek Salad	*Onion Soup	*Lentil Soup	*Chicken Consommé with Eggs	*Creamy Cucumber Salad	Green Salad
	Grilled Calves' Liver	*Marinated Chicken Tournedos	*John Dory with Romano Cheese	*Mushroom Omelette Soufflé	Tuna Salad	Chicken Salad	*Pork & Bean Sprouts
	*Cauliflower & Zucchini Curry	*Grilled Zucchini	Spinach	Tomatoes & Cucumbers		Vegetable Stir Fry	
	Cheese	Cheese	*Chocolate Mousse	Cheese	*Raspberry Cheesecake	Cheese	*English Custard
D I N N E R	Cream of Mushroom Soup	*Minestrone	Green Salad	*Rainbow Salad	Tomato Salad	*Cream of Spinach Soup	Vegetable Soup
	*Turbot Fillets Stuffed with Shrimp	*Rice & Lentils	*Turkey Scallops with Dijon Mustard	*Herbed Lentils & Tomatoes	*Scrambled Eggs & Ham	*Millet & Vegetable Salad	*Seafood Brochettes
	*Ratatouille		*Leeks in Cream				
	Unsweetened Dark Chocolate with 70% (Min.) Cocoa	**Yogurt	Yogurt	*Coconut Mounds	Yogurt	*Frozen Chocolate Yogurt	Yogurt

* See recipe.
** Flavour with unsweetened fruit jam or unsweetened apple sauce.

26

MENUS: WEEK 10

	MONDAY	TUESDAY	WEDNESDAY	THURSDAY	FRIDAY	SATURDAY	SUNDAY
L U N C H	*Avocado Salad *Cajun Veal Stew *Raspberry Bavarian Cream	*Cream of Spinach Soup *Stuffed Chicken Scallops *Red & Yellow Pepper Medley Cheese	Crudités with *Salsa *Tomatoes Stuffed with Eggs Cheese	*Chicken Consommé with Eggs Salmon Salad Cheese	*Alfalfa Sprout Salad *Andalusian Red Peppers & Beef Cheese	Green Salad *Mushroom Omelette Soufflé Unsweetened Dark Chocolate with 70% (Min.) Cocoa	Tomato Salad Grilled Haddock Steamed Cauliflower Cheese
D I N N E R	*Minestrone *Tabbouleh **Yogurt	*Caesar Salad *Lemon Coriander Tuna Brochettes *Lemon Sorbet	Cream of Vegetable Soup *Chicken Breasts with Orange & Ginger Steamed Vegetables Unsweetened Dark Chocolate with 70% (Min.) Cocoa	*Spinach & Bean Sprout Salad *Vegetarian Chili **Yogurt	Green Salad *Stuffed Rainbow Trout Green & Yellow Beans *Pears Poached in Wine	*Onion Soup *Herbed Lentils & Tomatoes **Yogurt	*Cream of Cauliflower Soup *Stuffed Zucchini Yogurt

* See recipe.
** Flavour with unsweetened fruit jam or unsweetened apple sauce.

MENUS: WEEK 11

	MONDAY	TUESDAY	WEDNESDAY	THURSDAY	FRIDAY	SATURDAY	SUNDAY
LUNCH	Crudités	Vegetable Soup	*Shrimp & Hearts of Palm Salad	*Italian Garden Salad	Hearts of Palm	Barley Soup	Tomato Salad
	*Stuffed Green Peppers	Grilled Chicken	*Scallop Gratin	*Turbot Fillets Stuffed with Shrimp	*Lamb Meatballs with Parmesan Sauce	*Stuffed Chicken Scallops	*Mexican Omelette
		*Ratatouille		*Leeks in Cream	Broccoli & Cauliflower	Sautéed Mushrooms	
	*Frozen Chocolate Yogurt	Cheese	*English Custard	Cheese	Unsweetened Dark Chocolate with 70% (Min.) Cocoa	*Strawberry Mousse	Cheese
DINNER	Cream of Mushroom Soup	Green Salad	Crudités	*Cold Cream of Asparagus Soup	Crudités	*Rainbow Salad	Cabbage Soup
	*Red Pepper & Black Olive Frittata	Wholewheat Pasta with *Lentil Sauce	Turkey in White Wine Sauce	*Wild Rice Salad	*Poached Fish	*Stuffed Eggplant	*Sole en Papillote
	Steamed Vegetables		*Grilled Zucchini		*Crisp Vegetables in Sour Cream		*Green Peas & Pearl Onions
	Yogurt	*Raspberry Snow	Yogurt	*Coconut Custard with Berries	Yogurt	***Yogurt	Unsweetened Dark Chocolate with 70% (Min.) Cocoa

* See recipe.
** Flavour with unsweetened fruit jam or unsweetened apple sauce.

MENUS: WEEK 12

	MONDAY	TUESDAY	WEDNESDAY	THURSDAY	FRIDAY	SATURDAY	SUNDAY
LUNCH	*Avocado Salad	Steamed Mussels	Watercress Salad	Green Salad	Leek & Watercress Soup	*Rainbow Salad	*Alfalfa Sprout Salad
	*Marinated Pork Chops	*Indian-Style Chicken	*Mexican Omelette	*Ginger Salmon	Calves' Liver	*Chicken Croquettes	*Trout Surprise
	Broccoli	*Cauliflower & Zucchini Curry		*Green Peas & Pearl Onions	Green & Yellow Beans	Broccoli	*Red & Yellow Pepper Medley
	Cheese	Unsweetened Dark Chocolate with 70% (Min.) Cocoa	*Raspberry Cheesecake	Cheese	*Lemon Sorbet	*Crème Brûlée	Cheese
DINNER	Shredded Carrot Salad	Vegetable Soup	Leek Soup	*Cream of Spinach Soup	Cucumber & Tomato Salad	*Minestrone	Vegetable Soup
	*Cheese & Spinach Rolls	*Salmon Tidbits	Grilled Cornish Hen	*Mediterranean Stew	*Broccoli Omelette	*Rice & Lentils	*Pork & Bean Sprouts
	Steamed Vegetables	*Leeks in Cream	*Ratatouille				
	*Raspberry & Almond Delight	Yogurt	Yogurt	Unsweetened Apple Sauce	Yogurt	**Yogurt	*Raspberry Snow

* See recipe.
** Flavour with unsweetened fruit jam or unsweetened apple sauce.

29

SOUPS

CHICKEN CONSOMMÉ WITH EGGS

SERVES 4

INGREDIENTS

- 4 cups (1 L) homemade defatted chicken stock (see p. 78)
- 3 green onions, thinly sliced
- 2 large eggs
- 1 Tbsp (15 mL) finely chopped fresh parsley
- 1 tsp (5 mL) tamari sauce (optional)
- Pinch celery salt
- Freshly ground black pepper to taste

- Bring to boil chicken stock. Add green onions and cook over medium heat 1 minute.

- In a bowl, beat eggs together with parsley, tamari and seasonings. Add to the chicken stock, stirring quickly, and continue cooking 1 minute longer.

- Serve immediately.

COLD CREAM OF ASPARAGUS SOUP

SERVES 2 TO 3

INGREDIENTS

- 2 lb (900 g) green asparagus, peeled
- 1 medium onion, thinly sliced
- 3 cups (750 mL) homemade defatted chicken stock (see p. 78)
- 1/2 cup (125 mL) plain yogurt
- Pinch celery salt
- Pinch cayenne pepper

- Cut asparagus into 1-inch (2.5 cm) pieces. Place in saucepan along with onion and stock, and bring to boil. Reduce heat and simmer, covered, 15 minutes.

- In a blender or food processor, purée mixture. Push mixture through a sieve to remove any fibrous parts. Transfer to blender and add yogurt. Season with celery salt, cayenne pepper and process until well blended. Check seasoning. Refrigerate 2 to 3 hours before serving.

CREAM OF
CAULIFLOWER SOUP

SERVES 4

INGREDIENTS

- 3 Tbsp (45 mL) olive oil
- 1 medium onion, thinly sliced
- 1 small head cauliflower cut into florets
- 3 Tbsp (45 mL) finely chopped fresh parsley
- 2 cups (500 mL) water
- 1 cup (250 mL) homemade defatted chicken stock (see p. 78)
- 1 cup (250 mL) 15% m.f. cream
- Salt and pepper to taste

- In a saucepan, over low heat, heat olive oil. Add onion and cook about 3 minutes. Add cauliflower and parsley. Cover partially and cook 8 to 10 minutes more.

- Add water and stock and bring to boil. Cover partially and simmer 5 minutes.

- Pour mixture into a blender or food processor, and purée while adding the cream. Return to stove and simmer a few minutes, or until mixture is creamy and homogenous. Season with salt and pepper, and serve.

CREAM OF SPINACH SOUP

SERVES 4

INGREDIENTS

- 1 Tbsp (15 mL) olive oil
- 1 medium onion, finely chopped
- 1 small clove garlic, peeled and crushed
- 7 oz (200 g) fresh spinach, washed, trimmed and patted dry with paper towels
- 2 cups (500 mL) water *or* homemade defatted chicken stock (see p. 78)
- 2 cups (500 mL) 15% m.f. cream
- Salt and pepper to taste

- In a saucepan, over low heat, heat olive oil. Add onion and garlic, and cook 2 minutes. Add spinach and cook 2 minutes more, stirring continuously.

- Add water or stock and bring to boil. Partially cover, and simmer 5 minutes.

- Transfer to a blender or food processor, and purée while adding the cream. Return to stove and simmer a few minutes until mixture is creamy. Season with salt and pepper before serving.

CREAMY TOMATO-YOGURT SOUP

SERVES 4

INGREDIENTS

- 2 cups (500 mL) tomato sauce with no sugar added
- 1 cup (250 mL) plain 0.1% m.f. yogurt
- 1 small clove garlic, peeled and crushed
- 1 Tbsp (15 mL) finely chopped fresh parsley
- 1/2 tsp (2 mL) dried basil
- 1/4 tsp (1 mL) onion powder
- Pinch cayenne pepper
- Salt to taste

- In a saucepan, place tomato sauce, yogurt, garlic and seasonings. Stir well and cook over very low heat about 15 minutes, stirring occasionally.

FISH SOUP

SERVES 4

INGREDIENTS

- 1 tsp (5 mL) olive oil
- 1 large clove garlic, peeled and crushed
- 1 medium onion, chopped
- 3 cups (750 mL) homemade defatted chicken stock (see p. 78)
- 1 cup (250 mL) crushed tomatoes
- 1/2 cup (125 mL) diced celery
- 1/2 cup (125 mL) diced zucchini
- 1/4 fresh fennel bulb, chopped
- 1 tsp (5 mL) grated fresh ginger
- 2 cups (500 mL) spinach leaves, washed, stems removed, torn into pieces
- 2 Tbsp (30 mL) tamari sauce
- 1/2 lb (250 g) white fish fillets, cut into large pieces
- Salt and pepper to taste

- In a saucepan, over low heat, heat olive oil, add garlic and onion and cook 2 to 3 minutes.

- Add stock and tomatoes, and bring to boil. Add celery, zucchini, fennel and ginger. Partially cover and cook over medium heat 5 minutes.

- Add spinach, tamari and fish, season with salt and pepper, and stir. Cook 10 minutes longer, or until fish turns opaque and flakes easily when tested with a fork.

LENTIL SOUP

SERVES 4 TO 6

INGREDIENTS

- 1 tsp (5 mL) olive oil
- 1 medium onion, chopped
- 1 stick celery, diced
- 1/2 small zucchini, diced
- 4 cups (1 L) homemade defatted chicken stock (see p. 78)
- 3 cups (750 mL) crushed tomatoes with their juice
- 1 large clove garlic, peeled and crushed
- 3 Tbsp (45 mL) finely chopped fresh parsley
- 3 Tbsp (45 mL) finely chopped fresh chives
- 1/2 tsp (2 mL) celery salt
- Pepper to taste
- 3 cups (750 mL) cooked green lentils
  (see cooking method, p. 220)

- In a large saucepan, over low heat, heat olive oil and cook onion, celery and zucchini 5 minutes.

- Add stock, tomatoes, garlic and seasonings. Cover, and cook over medium heat 10 minutes, stirring occasionally. Add lentils, and cook 2 minutes longer.

MEAL-IN-ONE SOUP

SERVES 4

INGREDIENTS

- 1 Tbsp (15 mL) olive oil
- 1/2 lb (225 g) beef rump, cut into small cubes
- 1 medium onion, chopped
- 1 small clove garlic, peeled and crushed
- 3 Tbsp (45 mL) finely chopped cilantro
- 2 tsp (10 mL) grated fresh ginger
- 1/2 tsp (2 mL) cumin powder
- 1/4 tsp (1 mL) celery salt
- Pinch cayenne pepper
- 1 cup (250 g) diced tomatoes
- 2 Tbsp (30 mL) tomato paste
- 5 cups (1.25 L) homemade defatted chicken stock (see p. 78)
- 1 cup (250 mL) cooked green lentils (see cooking method, p. 220)
- 1 cup (250 mL) cooked chickpeas (see cooking method, p. 220)
- Salt and freshly ground pepper to taste

- In a heavy saucepan, over medium heat, heat olive oil and brown meat about 2 minutes. Add onion, and cook about 5 more minutes.

- Add garlic, seasonings, tomatoes, tomato paste and stock. Bring to boil, reduce heat, cover and simmer 30 minutes.

- Add lentils and chickpeas. Season with salt and pepper. Stir well, and continue cooking 5 minutes.

MINESTRONE

SERVES 4

INGREDIENTS

- 1 Tbsp (15 mL) olive oil
- 1 medium onion, chopped
- 5 cups (1.25 L) homemade defatted chicken stock (see p. 78)
- 1 stick celery, diced
- 1/2 cup (125 mL) wax beans cut into 1/2-inch (1 cm) pieces
- 1 1/2 cups (375 mL) crushed tomatoes
- 1 Tbsp (15 mL) finely chopped fresh parsley
- 1 tsp (5 mL) finely chopped fresh basil
- 1/2 tsp (2 mL) dried oregano
- 1/2 tsp (2 mL) celery salt
- 1 small zucchini, diced
- 2 cloves garlic, peeled and crushed
- 1/2 cup (125 mL) wholewheat elbow macaroni
- 1 cup (250 mL) cooked red kidney beans
  (see cooking method, p. 220)

- In a saucepan, over medium heat, heat olive oil, add onion and cook 2 to 3 minutes.

- Add stock, celery, wax beans, tomatoes, parsley, basil, oregano and celery salt. Mix well, and bring to boil. Lower heat and simmer, uncovered, 15 minutes to reduce liquid.

- Stir in zucchini, garlic, macaroni. Cover, and cook 10 to 12 minutes more. Add red kidney beans and stir well. Simmer 2 minutes, and serve.

ONION SOUP

SERVES 4

INGREDIENTS

- 4 large onions, thinly sliced
- 4 cups (1 L) homemade defatted beef stock (see p. 77)
- 1/2 cup (125 mL) dry white wine
- Salt and pepper to taste
- 2 small slices wholewheat bread, toasted
- 1 cup (250 mL) grated Emmenthal or partially skimmed Gruyère cheese

- In a saucepan, bring onions and stock to boil. Lower the heat and simmer 20 minutes. Add wine and simmer 5 minutes longer. Season with salt and pepper.

- Preheat broiler.

- Pour the mixture into ovenproof soup bowls, cover each with a slice of toast and grated cheese. Broil until golden, 8 to 10 minutes.

PEA SOUP

SERVES 4

INGREDIENTS

- 1 cup (250 mL) whole yellow peas
- 1 Tbsp (15 mL) olive oil
- 1 stick celery, finely sliced
- 1 medium onion, finely chopped
- 3 cups (750 mL) homemade defatted chicken stock (see p. 78)
- 2 cups (500 mL) cold water
- 1 clove garlic, peeled and crushed
- 1/4 cup (50 mL) diced ham
- 1 Tbsp (15 mL) finely chopped fresh parsley
- Salt and pepper to taste

- Rinse peas thoroughly, and soak in cold water 10 to 12 hours.

- In a saucepan, over low heat, heat olive oil and cook onion and celery.

- Rinse and drain the soaked peas, and add to saucepan. Add water, cover and simmer 45 to 60 minutes, or until peas are soft.

SALADS

ALFALFA SPROUT SALAD

SERVES 4

INGREDIENTS

- 1 head Boston lettuce
- 2 cups (500 mL) alfalfa sprouts
- 1 very ripe tomato, quartered
- 1 pickling cucumber, thinly sliced
- 2 green onions, thinly sliced
- Salad dressing (see p. 57)

- Wash and dry lettuce, tear into pieces and place in a salad bowl.

- Add rest of ingredients and mix well. Serve with dressing on the side.

AVOCADO SALAD

SERVES 4 TO 6

INGREDIENTS

- 1 head curly red lettuce
- 2 ripe avocados, peeled and quartered
- 1 ripe tomato, quartered
- 2 green onions, thinly sliced
- Dijon mustard vinaigrette (see p. 62)

- Wash and dry lettuce and tear into pieces. Place in a salad bowl with the rest of the ingredients and mix well. Serve with dressing on the side.

CAESAR SALAD

SERVES 4

INGREDIENTS

- 1 head romaine lettuce
- 1 small slice toasted wholewheat bread, diced
- Caesar dressing (see p. 60)
- 1/4 cup (50 mL) freshly grated Parmesan cheese
- 4 slices bacon, cooked crisp and crumbled

- Wash and dry lettuce and tear into pieces. Place in a salad bowl and add diced bread. Add dressing and toss to coat leaves well. Sprinkle Parmesan and bacon bits over, and toss again.

CREAMY CUCUMBER SALAD

SERVES 3 TO 4

INGREDIENTS

- 4 fresh pickling cucumbers, peeled and sliced
- 1/4 cup (50 mL) plain yogurt
- 1/4 cup (50 mL) sour cream
- 1 Tbsp (15 mL) freshly squeezed lime juice
- 1 small clove garlic, peeled and crushed
- 1 Tbsp (15 mL) finely chopped fresh chives
- 1 Tbsp (15 mL) finely chopped cilantro
- 1/4 tsp (1 mL) celery salt
- Freshly ground black pepper to taste

- In a bowl, combine all ingredients. Refrigerate 1 hour, and serve.

GREEK SALAD

INGREDIENTS

- 2 ripe medium tomatoes, quartered
- 2 medium onions, quartered
- 7 oz (200 g) feta cheese, crumbled
- Balsamic vinaigrette (see p. 59)
- Calamata olives (amount optional)

- In a salad bowl, place tomatoes, onions and cheese, and mix well.

- Add vinaigrette and toss to coat well. Garnish with olives, and let sit 15 minutes before serving.

ITALIAN GARDEN SALAD

SERVES 4 TO 6

INGREDIENTS

- 1/2 head Boston or curly lettuce
- 1/2 head endive
- 1/2 bunch mache (lamb's lettuce)
- 1 small carrot, grated
- 2 ripe plum tomatoes, quartered
- 1/2 green pepper, cut into strips
- 4 radishes, thinly sliced
- 3 green onions, thinly sliced

ITALIAN DRESSING

- 1/4 cup (50 mL) grated romano cheese
- 1/3 cup (75 mL) extra-virgin olive oil
- 1 Tbsp (15 mL) freshly squeezed lime juice
- 1 large clove garlic, peeled and crushed
- 1 tsp (5 mL) dried basil
- 1 tsp (5 mL) dried oregano
- Salt and pepper to taste

- Wash lettuce, endive and mache. Tear into bite-size pieces. Add carrot, tomatoes, green pepper, radishes and green onions, and mix in a salad bowl.
- In a small bowl, whisk together dressing ingredients. Pour over salad, toss and serve.

RAINBOW SALAD

SERVES 4 TO 6

INGREDIENTS

- 1/2 head radicchio
- 1/2 head red-leafed lettuce
- 1/2 head Boston lettuce
- 1/2 Belgian endive
- 1/2 bunch watercress
- 1/2 yellow pepper, diced
- 1/4 cup (50 mL) finely chopped fresh parsley
- 1 Tbsp (15 mL) finely chopped fresh chives
- Dijon mustard vinaigrette (see p. 62)

- Wash and dry radicchio, red-leafed and Boston lettuce, endive and watercress. Tear into pieces and place in salad bowl.

- Add diced pepper, sprinkle with parsley and chives, and toss well. Serve with dressing on the side.

SHRIMP & HEARTS OF PALM SALAD

SERVES 4

INGREDIENTS

- 24 medium shrimp, cooked, shelled and deveined
- 1 can palm hearts, drained
- 2 ripe avocados, peeled and quartered
- 1 celery stick, thinly sliced
- 6 cherry tomatoes, cut in half
- Creamy vinaigrette (see p. 61)

- In a salad bowl, mix together all ingredients. Add enough vinaigrette to coat ingredients well, and toss. Let stand 10 minutes before serving.

SPINACH & BEAN SPROUT SALAD

SERVES 4

INGREDIENTS

- 1/3 lb (150 g) fresh spinach, stalks removed
- 2 cups (500 mL) bean sprouts
- 1/2 red pepper, cut into strips
- Tamari vinaigrette (see p. 64)

- Wash and dry spinach and sprouts. Tear spinach leaves and place in a salad bowl together with the sprouts and red pepper strips. Toss well. Drizzle with dressing and serve.

SPINACH & CARROT SALAD WITH ORANGE DRESSING

SERVES 4 TO 6

INGREDIENTS

- 1/3 lb (150 g) fresh spinach, stems removed
- 1/2 head Boston lettuce
- 1 large carrot, grated

DRESSING

- 1/4 cup (50 mL) sesame seed oil
- 2 Tbsp (30 mL) freshly squeezed orange juice
- 2 tsp (10 mL) freshly grated ginger
- 1 tsp (5 mL) freshly squeezed lemon juice
- 1 tsp (5 mL) grated orange zest
- 1/4 tsp (1 mL) Dijon mustard
- Salt and pepper to taste

- Wash and dry spinach and lettuce. Tear into bite-size pieces, place in a salad bowl and add carrot.

- In a small bowl, whisk together dressing ingredients. Serve on the side.

SUGAR PEAS & CURLY LETTUCE SALAD

SERVES 4 TO 6

INGREDIENTS

- 1/4 lb (125 mL) sugar peas
- 1 head curly lettuce *or* Boston lettuce
- 1/2 head escarole
- 1/2 head raddichio
- 1/2 red pepper, cut into thin strips
- Tamari vinaigrette (see p. 64)

- Shell sugar peas from pods and wash. Steam 2 minutes. Rinse in cold water and dry. Set aside.

- Wash and dry lettuce, escarole and raddichio. Tear and place in a salad bowl. Add peas and pepper strips, and toss. Serve with tamari vinaigrette on the side.

VINAIGRETTES
&
SALAD DRESSINGS

AROMATIC VINAIGRETTE

MAKES ABOUT 3/4 CUP (175 ML)

INGREDIENTS

- 1/2 cup (125 mL) extra-virgin olive oil
- 3 Tbsp (45 mL) freshly squeezed lime juice
- 1 1/2 Tbsp (22 mL) balsamic vinegar
- 1 Tbsp (15 mL) Dijon mustard
- 1 small clove garlic, peeled and crushed
- Salt and pepper to taste

- In a small bowl, whisk together all ingredients.

BALSAMIC VINAIGRETTE

MAKES 1 CUP (250 ML)

INGREDIENTS

- 3/4 cup (175 mL) extra-virgin olive oil
- 1/4 cup (50 mL) homemade defatted chicken stock (see p. 78)
- 3 Tbsp (45 mL) balsamic vinegar
- 2 Tbsp (30 mL) freshly squeezed lemon juice
- 1 large clove garlic, peeled and crushed
- 1 Tbsp (15 mL) finely chopped fresh oregano
- 1 Tbsp (15 mL) finely chopped fresh basil
- Salt and pepper to taste

- In bowl, whisk together all ingredients.

CAESAR DRESSING

MAKES 1/2 CUP (125 ML)

INGREDIENTS

- 1 large fresh egg yolk
- 2 Tbsp (30 mL) freshly squeezed lemon juice
- 1 large clove garlic, peeled and crushed
- 1/2 cup (125 mL) extra-virgin olive oil
- Salt and pepper to taste

- In a small bowl, beat egg yolk. Stir in lemon juice and garlic. Add oil in a thin, steady stream while beating continuously. Season with salt and pepper.

CREAMY VINAIGRETTE

MAKES ABOUT 3/4 CUP (175 ML)

INGREDIENTS

- 1 egg yolk
- 1 tsp (10 mL) Dijon mustard
- 1 tsp (10 mL) finely chopped fresh parsley
- Salt and pepper to taste
- 2 Tbsp (30 mL) freshly squeezed lemon juice
- 1/4 cup (50 mL) extra-virgin olive oil
- 1/4 cup (50 mL) cold-pressed sunflower oil
- 2 Tbsp (30 mL) sour cream

- In a small bowl, whisk together egg yolk, mustard and parsley. Season with salt and pepper, and add lemon juice.

- Add both oils in a thin stream while whisking continuously, then add sour cream.

DIJON MUSTARD VINAIGRETTE

MAKES 1/2 CUP (125 ML)

INGREDIENTS

- 1/2 cup (125 mL) extra-virgin olive oil
- 2 Tbsp (30 mL) Dijon mustard
- 1 1/2 Tbsp (22 mL) freshly squeezed lemon juice
- 1 large clove garlic, peeled and crushed
- 2 tsp (10 mL) finely chopped fresh parsley
- Salt and pepper to taste

- In a small bowl, whisk together all ingredients.

ROQUEFORT DRESSING

SERVES 4

INGREDIENTS

- 1/2 cup (125 mL) Roquefort or other blue cheese
- 1/4 cup (50 mL) plain yogurt or sour cream
- 2 Tbsp (30 mL) milk
- 2 tsp (10 mL) freshly squeezed lime juice
- Ground pepper to taste

- Blend all ingredients in a food processor until creamy. If too thick, add a little milk.

TAMARI VINAIGRETTE

MAKES 2/3 CUP (150 ML)

INGREDIENTS

- 1/2 cup (125 mL) homemade defatted chicken stock (see p. 78)
- 1-2 Tbsp (15-30 mL) tamari sauce
- Juice of half a small lemon
- 1 large clove garlic, peeled and crushed
- 1 Tbsp (15 mL) active dry yeast

- In a small bowl, whisk together all ingredients.

THREE OIL VINAIGRETTE

MAKES 1 CUP (250 ML)

INGREDIENTS

- 1/4 cup (50 mL) extra-virgin olive oil
- 1/4 cup (50 mL) cold-pressed sunflower oil
- 1/4 cup (50 mL) cold-pressed canola oil
- 1/4 cup (50 mL) freshly squeezed lemon juice
- 2 cloves garlic, peeled and crushed
- 1 Tbsp (15 mL) Dijon mustard
- 1 Tbsp (15 mL) finely chopped cilantro
- 1 Tbsp (15 mL) finely chopped fresh tarragon
- Salt and pepper to taste

- In a bowl, whisk together all ingredients.

SPREADS
&
DIPS

BRUSCHETTA

MAKES ABOUT 2/3 CUP (150 ML)

INGREDIENTS

- 2 medium very ripe tomatoes, deseeded and finely chopped
- 1 Tbsp (15 mL) finely chopped onion
- 1 large clove garlic, peeled and crushed
- 1 Tbsp (15 mL) extra-virgin olive oil
- 1 tsp (5 mL) freshly squeezed lemon juice
- 1/2 tsp (2 mL) balsamic vinegar
- 1 Tbsp (15 mL) pesto sauce
- 1 Tbsp (15 mL) finely chopped fresh parsley
- Salt and pepper to taste

- In a mixing bowl, whisk together all ingredients. Refrigerate 3 to 4 hours before using.

- *Serving suggestion:* Can be used as a sauce for meats, fish, legumes and rice.

CHICKPEA & SHRIMP DIP

MAKES ABOUT 1 1/2 CUPS (375 ML)

INGREDIENTS

- 2 cups (500 mL) cooked chickpeas
  (see cooking method, p. 220)
- 3/4 cup (175 mL) small cooked shrimp
- 2 Tbsp (30 mL) freshly squeezed lemon juice
- 2 Tbsp (30 mL) finely chopped cilantro
- 2 tsp (10 mL) extra-virgin olive oil
- 2 tsp (10 mL) finely chopped jalapeño or other hot red pepper
- Salt and pepper to taste

- In a blender or food processor, purée chickpeas, shrimp, lemon juice, cilantro, olive oil and hot pepper. If it gets too dry, add 1 to 2 Tbsp water.

- Season with salt and pepper, and process again.

- *Serving tip:* Use as dip for crudités, or spread on wholewheat crackers.

COTTAGE CHEESE SPREAD

MAKES ABOUT 1 CUP (250 ML)

INGREDIENTS

- 1 cup (250 mL) cottage cheese
- 3 Tbsp (45 mL) chopped red pepper
- 1 Tbsp (15 mL) finely chopped fresh parsley
- 2 tsp (10 mL) finely chopped fresh chives
- 1 tsp (5 mL) chopped jalapeño or similar hot pepper
- 1/4 tsp (1 mL) onion powder

- In a food processor or blender, place all ingredients and process until mixture is smooth and creamy. Check seasoning, and adjust if necessary.

- *Serving tip:* Serve on wholewheat crackers, or use as a dip for crudités.

HUMMUS

MAKES ABOUT 1 1/2 CUPS (375 ML)

INGREDIENTS

- 1 1/2 cups (375 mL) cooked chickpeas (see cooking method, p. 220)
- 1/3 cup (75 mL) plain yogurt
- 1 Tbsp (15 mL) extra-virgin olive oil
- 1 small clove garlic, peeled and crushed
- 1 Tbsp (15 mL) freshly squeezed lime juice
- 1 Tbsp (15 mL) finely chopped fresh mint
- 1/4 tsp (1 mL) curry powder
- 1/4 tsp (1 mL) celery salt
- Freshly ground black pepper

- Place all the ingredients into a blender or food processor, and purée.

- Serve on wholewheat crackers.

SALSA

MAKES 2 CUPS (500 ML)

INGREDIENTS

- 2 Tbsp (30 mL) extra-virgin olive oil
- 1 medium onion, diced
- 1/2 green pepper, diced
- 1 1/2 cups (375 mL) diced tomatoes
- 2 to 3 jalapeño or other hot peppers, deseeded and finely chopped
- 1 tsp (5 mL) red wine vinegar
- 2 Tbsp (30 mL) freshly chopped cilantro
- 1 Tbsp (15 mL) freshly chopped fresh parsley
- 1/2 tsp (2 mL) cumin powder
- 1/4 tsp (1 mL) celery salt
- Salt and freshly ground pepper to taste

- In a skillet, over low heat, heat 1 Tbsp of the olive oil; add onion and peppers, and cook 5 minutes. In a bowl, place remaining ingredients, including 1 Tbsp olive oil. Add cooked onion mixture, mix well and refrigerate 8 to 10 hours.

- Bring to room temperature before serving.

- *Serving suggestion:* Use as sauce for chicken, fish, rice and legumes.

TANGY DIP

MAKES ABOUT 1 CUP (250 ML)

INGREDIENTS

- 1/2 cup (125 mL) sour cream
- 1/4 cup (50 mL) plain yogurt
- 2 Tbsp (30 mL) finely chopped red onion
- 1 clove garlic, peeled and chopped
- 2 Tbsp (30 mL) finely chopped fresh chives
- 1 tsp (5 mL) finely chopped dill (optional)

- In a food container fitted with a tight lid, combine ingredients and store in refrigerator 45 minutes before serving.

- *Serving suggestion:* Can be served as a dip for vegetables and grilled meats.

TZATZIKI

MAKES 1 CUP (250 ML)

INGREDIENTS

- 3/4 cup (175 mL) sour cream
- 1/4 cup (50 mL) plain yogurt
- 2 Tbsp (30 mL) diced cucumber
- 2 large cloves garlic, peeled and crushed
- 1 Tbsp (15 mL) freshly squeezed lime juice
- 1 tsp (5 mL) extra-virgin olive oil
- 1/2 tsp (2 mL) balsamic vinegar
- 2 Tbsp (30 mL) finely chopped fresh parsley

- In a small bowl, whisk together all ingredients. Refrigerate at least 2 hours before serving.

- *Serving suggestion:* Can be served as a dip for vegetables and grilled meats.

SAUCES
&
STOCKS

GREEN DILL SAUCE

SERVES 4

INGREDIENTS

- 1 cup (250 mL) cottage cheese
- 1/4 cup (50 mL) plain yogurt
- 1/4 cup (50 mL) chopped fresh dill
- 2 Tbsp (30 mL) chopped fresh chives
- Salt and pepper to taste

- In a food processor or blender, process all ingredients until smooth. Serve at room temperature as a sauce for grilled fish.

HOMEMADE BEEF STOCK

MAKES ABOUT 5 CUPS (1.25 L)

INGREDIENTS

- 1 Tbsp (15 mL) olive oil
- 3 lb (1.35 kg) beef shins
- 6 cups (1.5 L) water
- 2 medium onions, coarsely chopped
- 1 celery stick with leaves, chopped
- 2 large cloves garlic, peeled and crushed
- 1/2 tsp (2 mL) dried Herbes de Provence
- Pinch mustard powder
- Salt and pepper to taste

- In a large saucepan, brown beef shins in olive oil. Add remaining ingredients and bring to boil. Cover and simmer 1 1/2 to 2 hours. Remove from heat and let cool 30 minutes.

- Using a fine-meshed colander, strain stock, cover and refrigerate. When stock is cold, skim fat off top using a spoon. Store in refrigerator up to 3 days, or freeze.

HOMEMADE CHICKEN STOCK

MAKES ABOUT 5 CUPS (1.25 L)

INGREDIENTS

- 1 large chicken carcass, preferably grain-fed, cut into pieces
- 6 cups (1.5 L) water
- 2 medium onions, quartered
- 3 celery sticks with leaves, coarsely chopped
- 1/2 turnip, cut into large pieces
- 2 large cloves garlic, peeled and crushed
- 1 Tbsp (15 mL) dried parsley
- 1/2 tsp (2 mL) dried Herbes de Provence
- 1 small bay leaf
- Salt and pepper to taste

- In a large saucepan, place all ingredients and bring to boil. Cover and simmer 1 1/2 to 2 hours. Remove from heat and let cool 30 minutes.

- Using a fine-meshed colander, strain stock and skim fat with a spoon. Store, covered, in refrigerator up to 3 days, or freeze.

LENTIL SAUCE

SERVES 6

INGREDIENTS

- 3 cups (750 mL) crushed tomatoes
- 3 cups (750 mL) tomato sauce
- 1/4 cup (50 mL) tomato paste
- 2 Tbsp (30 mL) olive oil
- 2 medium onions, coarsely chopped
- 1 celery stick, coarsely chopped
- 1 medium green pepper, coarsely chopped
- 1 tsp (5 mL) concentrated vegetable stock
- 1/2 Tbsp (7 mL) dried Herbes de Provence
- 1/4 tsp (1 mL) dried red pepper flakes
- Salt and pepper to taste
- 1 large clove garlic, peeled and crushed
- 1/2 cup (375 mL) cooked green lentils
  (see cooking method, p. 220)

- In a large saucepan, place crushed tomatoes, tomato sauce and tomato paste. Add olive oil and vegetables with the stock and seasonings. Mix well, cover and simmer 30 minutes, stirring occasionally.

- Add garlic, remove cover and cook over low heat 30 to 45 minutes.

- Add cooked lentils and simmer 15 minutes more.

PINK SAUCE WITH RED PEPPERS

MAKES ABOUT 3/4 CUP (175 ML)

INGREDIENTS

- 2 Tbsp (30 mL) olive oil
- 2 red peppers, cut into strips
- 1/2 medium onion, chopped
- 1 Tbsp (15 mL) freshly squeezed lime juice
- 1 Tbsp (15 mL) pesto sauce
- 1 clove garlic, peeled and crushed
- 2 tsp (10 mL) tamari sauce
- 1/4 tsp (1 mL) curry powder
- Pinch freshly ground black pepper
- 1/4 cup (50 mL) plain 0.1% m.f. yogurt

- In a large nonstick skillet, over medium heat, heat olive oil and cook peppers about 10 minutes.

- Add lime juice, pesto, garlic, tamari, curry powder and pepper, and continue to cook 6 to 7 minutes, stirring occasionally.

- In a blender or food processor, purée mixture while adding yogurt.

- *Serving suggestion:* Use as sauce for grilled fish or seafood.

TOFU TOMATO SAUCE

SERVES 4 TO 6

INGREDIENTS

- 7 cups (1.75 L) crushed tomatoes
- 1 1/4 cups (300 mL) tomato paste
- 2 large cloves garlic, peeled and crushed
- 1 1/2 Tbsp (22 mL) concentrated vegetable stock
- 2 tsp (10 mL) dried basil
- 1 tsp (5 mL) Herbes de Provence
- 1/2 lb (225 g) tofu
- 2 Tbsp (30 mL) olive oil

- In a saucepan, place tomatoes, tomato paste, garlic, stock, basil and Herbes de Provence. Cover and simmer about 30 minutes.

- In a blender or food processor, process tofu with 1/4 cup tomato sauce until well blended. Add to the tomato-herb mixture along with the olive oil and simmer, uncovered, 30 to 45 minutes longer.

TOMATO COULIS

MAKES ABOUT 1 1/2 CUPS (375 ML)

INGREDIENTS

- 1 tsp (5 mL) olive oil
- 1 small onion, chopped
- 5 large, very ripe tomatoes, peeled, deseeded and chopped
- 1 Tbsp (15 mL) tomato paste
- 1 Tbsp (15 mL) finely chopped fresh parsley
- 1/4 tsp (1 mL) powdered sage
- Pinch celery salt
- 1 1/2 cups (375 mL) homemade defatted chicken stock (see p. 78)
- Salt and freshly ground pepper to taste

- In a skillet, over medium heat, heat olive oil. Add onion and cook until transparent. Add rest of ingredients and cook over low heat 20 minutes. Check seasoning.

- In a blender or food processor, purée mixture. Serve hot or at room temperature.

- *Note:* To peel tomatoes, plunge into boiling water 30 seconds; skin will slide off easily.

MEAT

ANDALUSIAN RED PEPPERS & BEEF

SERVES 4

INGREDIENTS

- 1 lb (450 g) lean ground beef
- 3 Tbsp (45 mL) tamari sauce
- 1 Tbsp (15 mL) balsamic vinegar
- 4 medium red peppers, cut into strips
- Olive oil
- 1 small clove garlic, peeled and crushed
- 2 Tbsp (30 mL) freshly squeezed lime juice
- 1/4 tsp (1 mL) dried thyme
- 1/4 tsp (1 mL) curry powder
- Pinch onion powder
- Pepper to taste
- 3/4 lb (350 g) frozen green peas, defrosted

- In a nonstick pan, brown ground beef. Midway through cooking, add balsamic vinegar and 1/3 of the tamari sauce. Set aside.

- In a large saucepan, over medium heat, cook peppers in 1/4 cup olive oil for 3 minutes. Add garlic, half the lime juice and rest of the tamari sauce. Add seasonings and continue cooking until peppers are tender.

- To this mixture add browned beef, peas, rest of the lime juice and 2 Tbsp olive oil. Mix thoroughly, cover and cook over medium heat 20 to 25 minutes, stirring occasionally.

CAJUN VEAL STEW

SERVES 4

INGREDIENTS

- 3 Tbsp (45 mL) olive oil
- 1 lb (450 g) stewing veal, bones and fat removed
- 2 large cloves garlic, peeled and crushed
- 2 1/2 cups (625 mL) homemade defatted chicken stock (see p. 78)
- 12 small onions, peeled
- 1 Tbsp (15 mL) grated fresh ginger
- 2 tsp (10 mL) curry powder
- 1 tsp (5 mL) pesto sauce
- 1 tsp (5 mL) coriander powder
- Pinch cayenne pepper
- 3 Tbsp (45 mL) dry white wine
- 1 green pepper, cut into pieces
- 1 red pepper, cut into pieces
- 1 zucchini, cut into pieces
- 1/2 medium eggplant, cut into pieces
- 1/2 cup (125 mL) green beans, halved
- 1/2 cup (125 mL) wax beans, halved
- Salt and pepper to taste
- 2 Tbsp (30 mL) sour cream

- In a saucepan, over medium heat, brown veal on all sides in olive oil and crushed garlic.

- Add chicken stock, onions and seasonings. Stir, cover and simmer about 1 to 1 1/4 hours. Check occasionally, and add more stock if necessary.

- Add wine and vegetables. Season with salt and pepper, and mix well. Cover and cook 15 to 20 minutes more.

- Stir in sour cream, and serve.

CHILI CON CARNE

SERVES 4

INGREDIENTS

- 3 Tbsp (45 mL) olive oil
- 1 large onion, coarsely chopped
- 1/2 green pepper, coarsely chopped
- 1 celery stick, coarsely chopped
- 1 lb (450 g) lean ground beef
- 3 cloves garlic, peeled and crushed
- 2 tsp (10 mL) dried oregano
- 2 tsp (10 mL) cumin powder
- 1-2 tsp (5-10 mL) chili powder
- 5 cups (1.25 L) crushed tomatoes
- 2 tsp (10 mL) concentrated vegetable stock
- 1 tsp (5 mL) tamari sauce
- 2 cups (500 mL) cooked kidney beans
  (see cooking method, p. 220)

- In a skillet, over low heat, heat olive oil. Add onion, pepper and celery, and let cook about 5 minutes.

- Meanwhile, in a saucepan, brown the beef. Add onion mixture, garlic and seasonings to the meat. Stir well, and cook a few minutes over low heat.

- Add tomatoes, stock and tamari. Simmer 30 minutes more.

- Add cooked beans and continue cooking about 15 minutes more.

LAMB MEATBALLS WITH PARMESAN SAUCE

SERVES 6

INGREDIENTS

- 1 1/2 lb (675 g) lean ground lamb
- 1 medium onion, finely chopped
- 2 Tbsp (30 mL) oat bran
- 1/2 cup (125 mL) tomato juice
- 2 large cloves garlic, peeled and crushed
- 1 Tbsp (15 mL) dried Herbes de Provence
- Salt and pepper to taste

PARMESAN SAUCE

- 2 tsp (10 mL) olive oil
- 1 green onion, thinly sliced
- 1/4 cup (50 mL) dry white wine
- 1/2 cup (125 mL) 15% m.f. cream
- 3 Tbsp (45 mL) freshly grated Parmesan cheese
- 1 Tbsp (15 mL) finely chopped fresh parsley

- In a mixing bowl, combine lamb, onion, bran, tomato juice, garlic and seasonings. Refrigerate 30 minutes, then shape mixture into 6 meatballs.

- To make sauce, heat olive oil in a small saucepan over low heat, add green onion and cook until tender. Deglaze with wine, stir in cream and simmer 30 seconds. Add cheese and parsley, then whisk the sauce 2 minutes, or until it has a creamy consistency.

- In a nonstick pan, cook meatballs about 3 minutes on both sides. Serve with sauce on the side.

LAMB & VEGETABLE CASSEROLE

SERVES 2 TO 3

INGREDIENTS

- 2 tsp (10 mL) olive oil
- 1 lb (450 g) boned stew lamb
- 1 medium onion, quartered
- 1 cup (250 mL) homemade defatted beef stock (see p. 77)
- 2 cloves garlic, peeled and crushed
- 2 tsp (10 mL) curry powder
- 2 tsp (10 mL) dried Herbes de Provence
- 1 clove
- 1 cup (250 mL) diced tomatoes
- 1 Tbsp (15 mL) apple cider vinegar
- 1/4 head Savoy cabbage, rough chopped
- 1 small zucchini, cut into 1/2-inch (1 cm) slices
- 2 cups (500 mL) wax beans, cut in two
- 1 apple, peeled, cored and diced
- 3 Tbsp (45 mL) finely chopped fresh parsley
- 1 cup (250 mL) cooked green lentils
  (see cooking method, p. 220)
- Salt and pepper to taste

- Preheat oven to 350°F (180°C).

- In a dutch oven, over medium heat, heat olive oil; add onions and lamb and brown on all sides.

- Add stock, garlic, curry powder, dried herbs and clove. Cover, and bake 1 hour. If necessary, add a little stock during baking to prevent from drying.

- Add tomatoes, vinegar, cabbage, zucchini and wax beans, and stir. Bake, covered, 30 minutes longer, or until beans are crisp-tender.

- Add apple and parsley, and stir. Bake, covered, 15 minutes longer.

- Add lentils, season with salt and pepper, and bake 10 to 15 minutes longer.

MARINATED PORK CHOPS

SERVES 4

INGREDIENTS

- Olive oil
- 1 medium onion, finely chopped
- 6 medium very ripe tomatoes, peeled and coarsely chopped
- 1 large clove garlic, peeled and crushed
- 3 Tbsp (45 mL) pesto sauce
- 2 Tbsp (30 mL) freshly squeezed lime juice
- 1 tsp (5 mL) dried oregano
- 1 tsp (5 mL) dried tarragon
- 1 tsp (5 mL) celery salt
- 1/2 tsp (2 mL) coriander powder
- Salt and pepper to taste
- 8 pork chops, grilled

- Heat 2 Tbsp olive oil in a large saucepan; add onions and cook over low heat for 3 minutes.

- Add tomatoes together with 2 more Tbsp olive oil and the rest of the ingredients (except pork chops). Mix the sauce thoroughly, partially cover and simmer 1 to 1 1/2 hours, stirring occasionally. Refrigerate 10 to 12 hours.

- Spoon sauce onto grilled pork chops before serving.

- *Note:* To peel tomatoes, plunge into boiling water 30 seconds and remove; skin will peel off easily.

MEAT LOAF

SERVES 4 TO 6

INGREDIENTS

- 2 lb (900 g) lean ground beef
- 2 large eggs, beaten
- 1 1/4 cups (300 mL) tomato juice
- 3/4 cup (175 mL) rolled oats (quick-cooking, not instant)
- 1/4 cup (50 mL) wheat flakes
- Pinch black pepper
- Pinch dried sage
- Pinch dried basil
- 1/4 cup (50 mL) finely chopped onion

- Preheat oven to 350°F (180°C).

- In a large bowl, mix ground meat, eggs and tomato juice.

- Add oat and wheat flakes, seasonings and onion, and mix thoroughly.

- Transfer to a loaf pan, and bake 1 1/2 hours.

- *Suggestions:* Serve with bruschetta or pink sauce with red peppers (see recipes, pp. 68 and 80).

PORK & BEAN SPROUTS

SERVES 4

INGREDIENTS

- 2 Tbsp (30 mL) olive oil
- 1 medium onion, thinly sliced
- 1/2 leek, white part only, thinly sliced
- 1/3 green pepper, cut into strips
- 1 stalk celery, thinly sliced
- 1/4 cup (50 mL) sliced water chestnuts (optional)
- 1 lb (450 g) pork loin, bones and fat removed, cut into 1-inch (2.5 cm) slices
- 2 cups (500 mL) homemade defatted chicken stock (see p. 78)
- 3 Tbsp (45 mL) tamari sauce
- 5 cups (1.25 L) bean sprouts

- In a large saucepan, over low heat, heat olive oil, add onion, leek, celery and water chestnuts, and cook until tender. Add pork and brown 5 minutes.

- Add stock and tamari sauce, stir and bring to boil. Lower heat and simmer 10 minutes.

- Add sprouts, cover and cook 5 minutes more, stirring occasionally.

ROAST BEEF WITH RED WINE

SERVES 4 TO 6

INGREDIENTS

- 2 lb (900 g) roast beef, bone removed
- 2 cups water (500 mL) water
- 1/4 cup (80 mL) olive oil
- 1/4 cup (80 mL) tamari sauce
- 1 Tbsp (15 mL) strawberry vinegar
- 1 Tbsp (15 mL) cider vinegar
- 4 cloves garlic, peeled and crushed
- 1/2 tsp (2 mL) dried oregano
- 1/2 tsp (2 mL) dried parsley flakes
- 1/2 tsp (2 mL) dried thyme
- Freshly ground black pepper to taste
- 12 Brussels sprouts
- 1/2 lb (225 g) wax beans, cut in half
- 1/2 cup (125 mL) red wine

- Preheat oven to 350°F (180°C).

- In a casserole, place beef. Add water, olive oil, tamari, both vinegars, garlic and seasonings. Cover and bake 30 minutes.

- Add Brussels sprouts and wax beans, cover, and bake 30 minutes more.

- Remove and slice beef into 1/2-inch (1 cm) slices. Return to casserole, spreading slices around, pour wine over, and roast, uncovered, 30 to 45 minutes, or until vegetables are crisp-tender. If necessary, add a little water during the cooking to prevent from drying.

STUFFED GREEN PEPPERS

SERVES 4

INGREDIENTS

- 8 medium green peppers
- 3 Tbsp (45 mL) olive oil
- 10 green onions, thinly sliced
- 2 cups (500 mL) thinly sliced mushrooms
- 1 cup (250 mL) thinly sliced celery
- 1 lb (450 g) lean ground veal
- 2 cloves garlic, peeled and crushed
- 1 tsp (5 mL) dried Herbes de Provence
- 4 medium-size ripe tomatoes, diced
- 1 tsp (5 mL) undiluted vegetable stock
- 1/2 cup (75 mL) hot water
- Salt and pepper
- 3/4 cup (175 mL) cooked green lentils
  (see cooking method, p. 220)
- 1/2 cup (125 mL) freshly grated Parmesan cheese
- 1 cup (250 mL) part-skim grated mozzarella cheese

- Cut top off peppers, core and seed, and rinse well. Soak in hot water 4 minutes. Drain on paper towels and set aside.

- Preheat oven to 375°F (190°C).

- In a large skillet, heat olive oil and cook onions, mushrooms and celery over low heat 3 minutes. Add garlic and veal, and cook over medium heat until meat has browned.

- Add tomatoes and stock thinned with the hot water. Season with salt and pepper; stir, and simmer about 8 minutes.

- Add cooked lentils to the mixture and stir well. Fill each pepper halfway with the mixture and sprinkle with Parmesan. Fill peppers with remaining mixture and top with mozzarella.

- Place filled peppers in a baking dish, and bake about 15 minutes or until cheese is golden.

STUFFED ZUCCHINI

SERVES 4

INGREDIENTS

- 4 medium zucchini
- 1/4 lb (100 g) ground lean veal
- 2 tsp (10 mL) olive oil
- 1 small onion, chopped
- 1 small clove garlic, peeled and crushed
- 2 Tbsp (30 mL) finely chopped fresh parsley
- 1/2 tsp (2 mL) dried basil
- 1/2 tsp (2 mL) dried oregano
- Salt and freshly ground pepper to taste
- 1 cup (500 mL) chopped tomatoes
- 1/2 cup (125 mL) homemade defatted beef stock (see p. 77)
- 1 Tbsp (15 mL) dry red wine
- 1/2 cup (125 mL) cooked green lentils
  (see cooking method, p. 220)
- 1/4 cup (50 mL) freshly grated Parmesan cheese
- 1/4 cup (50 mL) freshly grated mozzarella cheese

- Cut zucchini in half, lengthwise, and scoop out pulp. Place zucchini halves in a baking dish. Reserve half the pulp.

- In a nonstick skillet, over medium heat, brown ground veal about 3 to 4 minutes. Transfer to a bowl.

- In the same skillet, heat olive oil, and cook onion, garlic and seasonings about 3 minutes. Add zucchini pulp, tomatoes, beef stock and wine, and cook about 15 minutes.

- Preheat oven to 375°F (190°C).

- Mix together meat, tomato mixture and lentils. Mix well and stuff zucchini halves with this mixture. Cover with combined grated cheeses, and bake 10 to 15 minutes, or until zucchini are tender.

VEAL BROCHETTES

SERVES 4

INGREDIENTS

- 1 1/2 lb (675 g) veal loin, bones and fat removed
- 16 small onions, peeled
- 1 medium zucchini, sliced into 1/2-inch (1 cm) pieces
- 16 cherry tomatoes

MARINADE

- 1/4 cup (50 mL) olive oil
- 1 Tbsp (15 mL) tamari sauce
- 2 Tbsp (30 mL) grated fresh ginger
- 2 tsp (10 mL) curry powder

- Cut the veal into 1-inch (2.5 cm) cubes.

- In a large bowl, mix marinade ingredients, reserving 1/4 for basting. Add veal and mix to coat well. Refrigerate about 3 hours.

- Boil onions in lightly salted water until tender.

- Preheat broiler.

- Thread marinated veal onto metal skewers, alternating with the vegetables. Baste onions, zucchini and tomatoes with rest of marinade.

- Place skewers into a shallow pan and broil about 15 minutes, turning over and basting halfway through cooking.

VEAL CHOPS WITH CHERVIL & CAPERS

SERVES 4

INGREDIENTS

- 1/3 cup (75 mL) olive oil
- 1 clove garlic, peeled and crushed
- 1 Tbsp (15 mL) finely chopped fresh parsley
- 1 Tbsp (15 mL) finely chopped fresh chives
- 2 tsp (10 mL) dried chervil
- 2 tsp (10 mL) chopped capers
- 1/2 Tbsp (7 mL) Dijon mustard
- 4 veal loin chops

- In a bowl, mix all ingredients, except veal, to make a marinade. Add veal chops, turning to coat well, and refrigerate at least 2 hours.

- In a nonstick skillet, over medium heat, cook veal chops in half the marinade, 4 to 5 minutes on each side. Serve immediately.

VEAL SCALLOPS
WITH WHITE WINE

SERVES 4

INGREDIENTS

- Olive oil
- 1 1/2 lb (675 g) veal scallops
- 1 medium onion, thinly sliced
- 2 large cloves of garlic, peeled and crushed
- 1 1/2 cups (375 mL) thinly sliced mushrooms
- 2 Tbsp (30 mL) freshly squeezed lime juice
- 2 tsp (10 mL) tamari sauce
- 2 tsp (10 mL) balsamic vinegar
- 1/4 cup (50 mL) dry white wine
- Salt and pepper to taste

- In a large skillet, brown veal in a little olive oil, 2 to 3 minutes on each side. Transfer to a platter and set aside.

- In the same skillet, over low heat, add 3 Tbsp olive oil, and cook onions and garlic 5 minutes. Add lime juice, tamari and vinegar, and cook 2 to 3 minutes more.

- Add wine and veal scallops to the mixture. Season with salt and pepper, mix well, cover and simmer 3 minutes.

VEAL SLIVERS WITH VEGETABLES

SERVES 4

INGREDIENTS

- 2 Tbsp (30 mL) olive oil
- 2 medium onions, finely chopped
- 1/2 green pepper, cut into strips
- 1 zucchini, thinly sliced
- 1/3 head cauliflower, separated into florets
- 1 cup (350 mL) thinly sliced mushrooms
- 1 lb (450 g) veal loin, bones and visible fat removed, cut into 1-inch (2.5 cm) slices
- 5 cups (1.25 L) crushed tomatoes
- 2 cloves garlic, peeled and crushed
- 3 Tbsp (45 mL) red wine vinegar
- 2 Tbsp (30 mL) Dijon mustard
- 1 tsp (5 mL) concentrated vegetable stock
- 1 tsp (5 mL) dried Herbes de Provence
- Salt and pepper to taste

- In a saucepan, over low heat, heat olive oil, add vegetables and cook a few minutes. Add veal and brown 5 minutes.

- Add tomatoes, garlic, vinegar, mustard and stock; season with herbs, salt and pepper. Stir well, and simmer about 30 minutes.

FOWL

CHICKEN BREASTS WITH ORANGE & GINGER

SERVES 4

INGREDIENTS

- 1/3 cup (75 mL) olive oil
- 2 Tbsp (30 mL) grated fresh ginger
- 2 tsp (10 mL) freshly squeezed orange juice
- 1/2 Tbsp (7 mL) grated orange zest
- 2 tsp (10 mL) sour cream
- 1/2 tsp (2 mL) aniseed
- 1 1/2 lb (675 g) chicken breasts, bones, fat and skin removed

- In a mixing bowl, whisk together marinade ingredients. Add chicken breasts, turning over to coat well, and marinate about 3 hours.

- In a large skillet, over medium heat, cook chicken breasts 5 to 6 minutes on each side or until cooked.

CHICKEN CACCIATORE

SERVES 4

INGREDIENTS

- 4 large chicken thighs, skin removed
- 1 tsp (5 mL) dried basil
- 1/2 tsp (2 mL) dried oregano
- 1/2 tsp (2 mL) celery salt
- 1/2 tsp (2 mL) onion powder
- 1 cup (250 mL) fresh mushrooms, thinly sliced
- 1 medium green pepper, roughly chopped
- 1/2 medium red pepper, roughly chopped
- 1 medium onion, thinly sliced
- 1 cup (250 mL) dry white wine
- 1/2 cup (125 mL) tomato paste
- 2 1/2 cups (625 mL) diced tomatoes in their juice
- 1 Tbsp (15 mL) olive oil
- 4 large cloves garlic, peeled and crushed
- 2 bay leaves
- Salt and freshly ground pepper to taste

- In a baking dish, place chicken thighs and season with half the basil, oregano, celery salt and onion powder. Add mushrooms, peppers and onion, scattering evenly over chicken.

- In a large bowl, whisk together wine and tomato paste until well blended. Add rest of ingredients and mix. Pour over chicken, cover with plastic wrap and refrigerate 10 to 12 hours.

- Preheat oven to 350°F (180°C).

- Remove plastic wrap, and replace with aluminum foil. Bake about 1 hour, or until chicken is no longer pink when tested with a fork. Remove bay leaves, stir sauce in pan and spoon over chicken before serving.

CHICKEN CROQUETTES

SERVES 2 TO 3

INGREDIENTS

- 1/2 lb ground chicken breast
- 1 large egg, beaten
- 1/4 cup (50 mL) freshly grated Parmesan cheese
- 2 Tbsp (30 mL) oat bran
- 1 large clove garlic, peeled and crushed
- 1 tsp (5 mL) dried Herbes de Provence
- 1 tsp (5 mL) nutmeg powder
- Salt and freshly ground pepper to taste
- Olive oil

- In a bowl, combine ground chicken, egg, Parmesan, bran, garlic and seasonings. Shape into 8 croquettes.

- Preheat oven to 425°F (220°C).

- Place croquettes on a baking sheet lightly greased with olive oil. Bake 12 to 15 minutes, or until chicken is no longer pink when tested with a fork. Broil a few minutes to finish cooking and croquettes are golden.

- *Serving suggestion:* Serve with salsa or pink sauce with red peppers (see pp. 72 and 80).

CHICKEN TOURNEDOS WITH MUSHROOMS

SERVES 4

INGREDIENTS

- 2 Tbsp (30 mL) balsamic vinegar
- 1 tsp (10 mL) freshly squeezed lime juice
- 1 tsp (10 mL) Dijon mustard
- 1 large clove garlic, peeled and crushed
- 4 chicken tournedos (rounds about 1/2-inch thick, wrapped in bacon strip and secured with a wooden toothpick)
- 1 Tbsp (15 mL) olive oil
- 2 cups (500 mL) quartered mushrooms
- 3 green onions, thinly sliced
- 1/3 cup (75 mL) homemade defatted chicken stock (see p. 78)
- 1/2 tsp (2 mL) dried thyme
- Freshly ground black pepper to taste

- In a bowl, combine 1 Tbsp of the vinegar with lime juice. Add mustard and garlic, and mix well. Add chicken, turning over to coat well, and marinate in refrigerator about 1 hour.

- In a nonstick skillet, over medium heat, heat 2 tsp of the olive oil, add chicken along with marinade, and cook 4 to 5 minutes on each side, or until meat is no longer pink when tested with a fork. Remove chicken, and keep in a warm place.

112

- In the same skillet, add 1 tsp olive oil, and cook mushrooms and green onions 1 minute. Add stock, thyme, pepper and rest of vinegar, and cook 4 to 5 minutes, or until mushrooms are tender.

- Spoon mushroom mixture over chicken tournedos, and serve.

INDIAN-STYLE CHICKEN

SERVES 4

INGREDIENTS

- 1/2 cup (125 mL) sour cream
- 2 Tbsp (30 mL) freshly squeezed lime juice
- 1 Tbsp (15 mL) olive oil
- 2 tsp (10 mL) Dijon mustard
- 1 1/2 Tbsp (22 mL) grated fresh ginger
- 1 tsp (5 mL) coriander powder
- 1/2 tsp (2 mL) saffron powder
- 1/4 tsp (1 mL) cumin powder
- Salt and pepper to taste
- 4 chicken breasts, bones, fat and skin removed

- In a shallow baking dish, combine all marinade ingredients. Add chicken, turning over to coat well. Marinate in refrigerator about 3 hours.

- Preheat oven to 350°F (180°C).

- Place baking dish containing chicken and marinade in oven, and bake about 35 minutes, or until chicken is no longer pink when tested with a fork. Then broil a few minutes until chicken is golden.

JAMBALAYA

SERVES 4

INGREDIENTS

- 3/4 cup (175 mL) brown basmati rice
- 1 Tbsp (15 mL) olive oil
- 1 lb (450 g) chicken breasts, bones, fat and skin removed, cut into 2-inch (5 cm) strips
- 1 medium red pepper, chopped
- 1/2 stick celery, chopped
- 1 medium onion, chopped
- 2 cloves garlic, peeled and crushed
- 1 tsp (5 mL) jalapeño or similar hot pepper, chopped
- 2 bay leaves
- 1 tsp (5 mL) chili powder
- 1 tsp (5 mL) dried thyme
- 1 tsp (5 mL) dried oregano
- 1/2 tsp (2 mL) celery salt
- Pinch ground black pepper
- 1 1/2 cups (375 mL) homemade defatted chicken stock (see p. 78)
- 3/4 cup (175 mL) diced tomatoes
- 1/2 lb (225 g) vegetarian frankfurters made with tofu, cut into approx. 1/2-inch (1 cm) slices
- 3/4 cup (175 mL) frozen peas, defrosted
- 1/2 lb (225 g) fresh medium shrimp, shelled and deveined

- Soak rice in cold water 3 hours. Drain and rinse; place in pot with 2 cups (500 mL) of water. Bring to a boil and reduce heat. Cook over low heat 25 minutes. Drain excess water. Set aside.

- In a large saucepan, over medium heat, heat olive oil, and cook chicken 3 to 4 minutes, or until golden. Transfer to a plate.

- In the same pan, over low heat, cook red pepper, celery, onion, garlic, jalapeño and seasonings 5 minutes, stirring occasionally.

- Add cooked rice and stir thoroughly. Add stock, tomatoes and chicken, and bring to boil. Lower heat, cover and simmer 15 minutes, stirring occasionally.

- Add tofu frankfurters, and continue cooking about 10 to 15 minutes. If necessary, add a little stock during cooking to prevent drying.

- Add peas and shrimp. Mix well, cover and continue cooking 5 minutes or until shrimp turn pink. Remove bay leaves, and serve.

MARINATED CHICKEN TOURNEDOS

SERVES 4

INGREDIENTS

- 2 Tbsp (30 mL) extra-virgin olive oil
- 2 Tbsp (30 mL) freshly squeezed lemon juice
- 2 Tbsp (30 mL) freshly squeezed lime juice
- 1 large clove garlic, peeled and crushed
- 1/4 tsp (1 mL) dried oregano
- 1/4 tsp (1 mL) cumin powder
- 1/4 tsp (1 mL) celery salt
- 1/4 tsp (1 mL) onion powder
- 4 chicken tournedos (rounds of about 3/4-inch thick, wrapped in bacon strip and secured with a wooden toothpick)

- In a bowl, whisk together all the ingredients, except chicken, to make a marinade. Add chicken, turning to coat well. Marinate in refrigerator at least 2 hours.

- Preheat oven to 375°F (190°C).

- Transfer chicken to a lightly oiled baking sheet; reserve marinade. Bake 30 to 40 minutes, or until chicken is no longer pink when tested with a fork. Turn and baste with marinade halfway through baking.

MOROCCAN-STYLE CHICKEN

SERVES 4

INGREDIENTS

- 3 Tbsp (30 mL) olive oil
- 2 medium onions, chopped
- 3 large cloves garlic, peeled and crushed
- 1 1/2 lb (675 g) chicken thighs, bones, fat and skin removed
- 1 lime, quartered
- 2 Tbsp (30 mL) freshly squeezed lime juice
- 1/2 cup (125 mL) finely chopped fresh parsley
- 1/2 cup (125 mL) finely chopped cilantro
- 2 tsp (10 mL) grated fresh ginger
- 1 tsp (5 mL) powdered saffron
- 1/2 tsp (2 mL) cumin powder
- 1/4 tsp (1 mL) celery salt
- 1/4 tsp (1 mL) cinnamon
- Salt and freshly ground pepper to taste
- 2 1/2 cups (625 mL) homemade defatted chicken stock (see p. 78)
- 1/4 cup (50 mL) pitted, sliced green olives
- 1/4 cup (50 mL) pitted, sliced black olives

- In a pan, over medium heat, heat olive oil. Brown onions, garlic and chicken on all sides.

- Add lime quarters, lime juice and seasonings. Add stock, and bring to boil. Cover, and cook over medium heat about 40 minutes, or until chicken is almost done. If necessary, add a little chicken stock to prevent from drying.

- Add olives, stir well and continue cooking 15 minutes more, or until chicken is no longer pink when tested with a fork.

ORIENTAL CHICKEN KEBABS

SERVES 4

INGREDIENTS

- 1 1/2 lb (675 g) chicken breasts, bones and skin removed
- 4 medium onions, quartered
- 2 medium green peppers, cut into medium-size pieces
- 2 leaves Chinese cabbage (bok choy), cut into medium-size pieces

MARINADE

- 1/3 cup (75 mL) sesame oil
- 1/3 cup (75 mL) homemade defatted chicken stock
- 1 1/2 Tbsp (22 mL) tamari sauce
- 1 Tbsp (15 mL) freshly squeezed lime juice
- 1 Tbsp (15 mL) grated fresh ginger
- 1 small clove garlic, peeled and crushed

- In a bowl, whisk marinade ingredients.

- Cut chicken into 1-inch (2.5 cm) cubes and add to marinade. Mix well to coat, and let marinate in refrigerator about 3 hours.

- Preheat broiler.

- Thread chicken pieces onto metal skewers, alternating chicken with the vegetables.

- Place skewers in a shallow pan and broil 15 minutes, or until chicken is cooked (test with a fork, meat should not be pink). Halfway through the cooking, turn and baste.

STUFFED CHICKEN SCALLOPS

SERVES 4

INGREDIENTS

- 1 1/2 lb (675 g) scalloped chicken slices
- 1 Tbsp (15 mL) olive oil
- 1 red or yellow pepper, cut into strips
- 1/3 lb (150 g) fresh spinach, washed, stalks trimmed
- 1 1/2 cups (375 mL) grated Swiss cheese
- 1/4 cup (50 mL) freshly grated Parmesan cheese
- 1/4 tsp (1 mL) dried thyme
- 1/4 tsp (1 mL) dried rosemary
- 1/4 tsp (1 mL) dried tarragon
- Pinch onion powder
- Salt and pepper to taste

MARINADE

- 1/3 cup (75 mL) olive oil
- 3 Tbsp (45 mL) freshly squeezed orange juice
- 3 Tbsp (45 mL) freshly squeezed grapefruit juice
- 2 Tbsp (30 mL) freshly squeezed lemon juice
- 2 Tbsp (30 mL) freshly squeezed lime juice
- 2 Tbsp (30 mL) Dijon mustard
- 2 large cloves garlic, peeled and crushed

- In a bowl, whisk together all the marinade ingredients. Add chicken scallops and turn to coat well. Marinate in refrigerator about 1 hour.

- Preheat oven to 350°F (180°C).

- In a nonstick skillet, over medium heat, heat olive oil and cook pepper strips 5 minutes. Add spinach, cover and continue cooking 1 to 2 minutes, or until spinach is wilted.

- Drain scallops and reserve marinade. Spoon spinach mixture and Swiss cheese onto each scallop, roll, and secure with a toothpick.

- On a plate, mix together Parmesan cheese, herbs and onion powder. Dip scallops in marinade, then roll lightly in Parmesan mixture. Season with salt and pepper.

- Transfer scallops to a baking dish and bake 20 minutes, or until chicken is no longer pink when tested with a fork.

TURKEY BREASTS
WITH APRICOTS

SERVES 4

INGREDIENTS

- 2 lb (900 g) turkey breasts, bones left in, skin removed
- Olive oil
- 1 Tbsp (15 mL) finely chopped fresh rosemary
- 3 Tbsp (45 mL) sugarless apricot spread
- 1 Tbsp (15 mL) sherry vinegar
- 2 tsp (10 mL) olive oil
- Salt and pepper to taste

- Preheat oven to 400°F (200°C).

- Season turkey with salt and pepper. Grease a baking dish with a little olive oil. Place turkey in baking dish, bone side up, and sprinkle with rosemary. Cover and bake 20 minutes.

- Meanwhile, whisk together rest of rosemary, apricot spread, vinegar and olive oil. Season with salt and pepper.

- Turn over turkey breasts, and baste with apricot mixture. Continue baking 20 to 25 minutes more, or until turkey is no longer pink when tested with a fork.

TURKEY CRACKLING

SERVES 4

INGREDIENTS

- 3/4 lb (350 g) ground lean turkey
- 1/2 medium onion, chopped
- 1 clove garlic, peeled and crushed
- 1 egg, beaten
- 1 cup (250 mL) milk
- 1/2 tsp (2 mL) dried Herbes de Provence
- 1/8 tsp (0.5 mL) ground cloves
- 1/8 tsp (0.5 mL) ground nutmeg
- 1 Tbsp (15 mL) finely chopped fresh parsley
- 1 Tbsp (15 mL) finely chopped fresh chives (optional)
- Salt and freshly ground pepper to taste

- In a bowl, combine all ingredients. Place in a pan, cover and cook over low heat about 1 1/2 hours, or until liquid has evaporated, stirring occasionally. Remove from heat and let cool about 30 minutes.

- Transfer mixture to a mould, pat down with a spatula to a thickness of about 1 inch (2.5 cm), and refrigerate about 1 1/2 hours.

- *Serving suggestion:* Serve with wholewheat crackers and Dijon mustard.

TURKEY WITH PEAS & TOMATOES

SERVES 2 TO 3

INGREDIENTS

- 1 Tbsp (15 mL) olive oil
- 1 small onion, chopped
- 1 lb (450 g) lean ground turkey
- 1 small clove garlic, peeled and crushed
- 1 tsp (5 mL) dried Herbes de Provence
- 1 tsp (5 mL) dried thyme
- 1/2 tsp (2 mL) curry powder
- 1 Tbsp (15 mL) tamari sauce
- 1/2 cup (125 mL) homemade defatted chicken stock (see p. 78)
- 1/2 lb (225 g) frozen peas, defrosted
- 1/2 cup (125 mL) diced tomatoes

- In a nonstick saucepan, over medium heat, heat olive oil, add onion and cook about 3 minutes. Add turkey and continue cooking 10 minutes, stirring occasionally.

- Add garlic, seasonings and tamari. Mix well and cook 2 minutes more.

- Add stock and peas, cover and continue cooking 5 minutes. Add tomatoes, and cook 5 minutes more, uncovered, stirring occasionally.

TURKEY SCALLOPS WITH DIJON MUSTARD

SERVES 4

INGREDIENTS

- 2 Tbsp (30 mL) freshly squeezed lime juice
- 1 tbsp (15 mL) Dijon mustard
- 1 clove garlic, peeled and crushed
- 1 tsp (5 mL) dried tarragon
- Salt and freshly ground pepper to taste
- 1 1/2 lb (675 g) scalloped turkey slices
- 1 Tbsp (15 mL) olive oil

- In a bowl, whisk lime juice, mustard, garlic and seasonings. Add turkey slices and turn to coat well. Marinate in refrigerator about 2 hours.

- In a large nonstick skillet, over medium heat, heat olive oil, cook turkey slices 3 to 4 minutes on each side, or until meat is no longer pink when tested with a fork.

TURKEY SCALLOPS WITH HERBS & SOUR CREAM

SERVES 4

INGREDIENTS

- 1/3 cup (75 mL) sour cream
- 1/4 cup (50 mL) homemade defatted chicken stock (see p. 78)
- 1/4 cup (50 mL) freshly squeezed lime juice
- 3 Tbsp (45 mL) olive oil
- 2 large cloves garlic, peeled and thinly sliced
- 2 tsp (10 mL) Dijon mustard
- 1 Tbsp (15 mL) finely chopped fresh chives
- 1 Tbsp (15 mL) dried Herbes de Provence
- Salt and pepper to taste
- 1 1/2 lb (675 g) turkey scallops (thin, flattened slices)

- In a mixing bowl, whisk all marinade ingredients. Add turkey and turn to coat well. Marinate in refrigerator about 2 hours.

- In a large nonstick skillet, over medium heat, cook turkey 2 to 3 minutes on each side, or until turkey is cooked through and meat is no longer pink when tested with a fork.

Fish Soup

- Page 37 -

Italian Garden Salad

- Page 51 -

Spinach & Carrot Salad
with Orange Dressing
- Page 55 -

Chickpea & Shrimp Dip
- Page 69 -

Lentil Sauce

- Page 79 -

Stuffed Zucchini

- Page 100 -

Moroccan-Style Chicken
- Page 118 -

Ginger Salmon
- Page 133 -

**Lemon Coriander
Tuna Brochettes**
- Page 136 -

Spicy Shrimp with Ginger
- Page 149 -

Red Pepper & Black Olive
Frittata
- Page 159 -

Lemon Dill Lentil
& Chikpea Salad
- Page 181 -

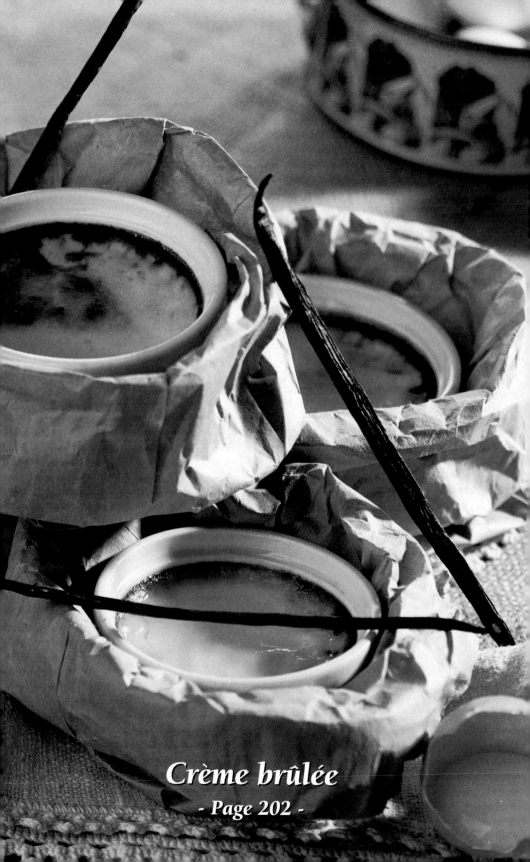

Crème brûlée
- Page 202 -

Lemon Sorbet

- Page 209 -

Raspberry Bavarian Cream
- Page 213 -

Michel Montignac's whole-grain breads, bagels and cakes are available at your local fine-food stores.

FISH
&
SEAFOOD

BROILED TUNA STEAKS

SERVES 4

INGREDIENTS

- 1 1/2 cups (375 mL) unsweetened coconut juice
- 1/4 cup (50 mL) freshly squeezed lime juice
- 2 jalapeño or other similar hot peppers, chopped
- 3 large cloves garlic, peeled and crushed
- 2 tsp (10 mL) paprika
- 1 tsp (5 mL) turmeric powder
- 1/2 tsp (2 mL) onion powder
- 1/4 tsp (1 mL) celery salt
- 4 tuna steaks

- Mix all ingredients, except tuna steaks, to make a marinade. Add tuna, turning over to coat well. Marinate in refrigerator 5 hours, turning tuna over occasionally.

- Preheat broiler.

- Transfer tuna to a shallow baking dish, and broil about 4 minutes on each side, or until fish is opaque and flakes easily when tested with a fork.

FISH FILLETS WITH TOMATO SAUCE & RED PEPPERS

SERVES 4

INGREDIENTS

- 2 Tbsp (30 mL) olive oil
- 1 medium red pepper, cut into strips
- 1 small onion, thinly sliced
- 1/2 cup (125 mL) dry white wine
- 1/4 cup (50 mL) homemade defatted chicken stock (see p. 78)
- 2 medium tomatoes, peeled, deseeded and chopped
- 1 small clove garlic, peeled and crushed
- 1/2 tsp (2 mL) dried Herbes de Provence
- 1/4 tsp (1 mL) celery salt
- 1/8 tsp (0.5 mL) curry powder
- Salt and freshly ground pepper to taste
- 4 white fish fillets, about 250 g each
- 1/4 cup (50 mL) 15% m.f. cream

- In a large nonstick skillet, over medium heat, heat olive oil and cook pepper strips and onion about 15 minutes.

- Add wine, stock, tomatoes, garlic and seasonings. Mix well. Add fish, cover and cook gently over medium-low heat about 8 minutes, or until fish is opaque and flakes when tested with a fork.

- Remove fish and keep warm.

- Add cream to tomato-pepper mixture, stirring continuously about 5 minutes, or until sauce thickens.

- Serve fish fillets with sauce on the side.

- *Note:* To peel tomatoes, place in boiling water 30 seconds. Skin will peel off easily.

GINGER SALMON

SERVES 4

INGREDIENTS

- 4 salmon fillets
- 2 medium onions, sliced
- 1 fresh lemon, sliced
- 1 large piece ginger, thinly sliced
- 1/2 cup (125 mL) vegetable stock
- Salt and pepper to taste
- Fresh parsley, finely chopped, to taste

- Wipe fillets with a paper towel, and place each one on a separate sheet of aluminum foil about 15 inches (40 cm) long.

- Preheat oven to 425°F (220°C).

- Top fillets with onion, lemon and ginger slices. Pour 2 Tbsp stock over. Season with salt, pepper and parsley. Fold aluminum foil over fillets, turn edges in and pinch to seal.

- Bake 15 to 20 minutes, or until fish is opaque and flakes easily when tested with a fork.

HADDOCK FILLETS WITH ALMONDS

SERVES 4

INGREDIENTS

- 1/2 cup (125 mL) ground almonds
- 1/4 tsp (1 mL) ground black pepper
- 1/4 tsp (1 mL) paprika
- 1 Tbsp (15 mL) finely chopped fresh parsley
- 1 tsp (5 mL) finely chopped fresh dill
- 4 haddock fillets
- 2 Tbsp (30 mL) olive oil
- 2 Tbsp (30 mL) freshly squeezed lemon juice

- In a plate, mix together almonds, pepper, paprika, parsley and dill. Dredge fillets in mixture, turning over to coat on both sides.

- In a skillet, over medium-high heat, heat olive oil, and cook fillets 2 to 3 minutes on each side. Sprinkle lime juice over, and continue cooking 1 minute on each side, or until fish is opaque and flakes easily when tested with a fork.

JOHN DORY WITH ROMANO CHEESE

SERVES 4

INGREDIENTS

- 1/2 cup (125 mL) freshly grated Romano cheese
- Freshly ground black pepper to taste
- 1 tsp (5 mL) dried garlic flakes
- 4 fillets of John Dory
- 2 Tbsp (30 mL) olive oil
- Juice of a fresh lemon

- Combine Romano, pepper and garlic, and coat fish fillets on both sides.

- In a skillet, over medium heat, heat olive oil and cook fillets 3 to 4 minutes on each side. Serve with lemon juice.

LEMON CORIANDER TUNA BROCHETTES

SERVES 4

INGREDIENTS

- 1 1/2 lb (675 g) fresh tuna steaks
- 16 cherry tomatoes
- 2 small red onions, quartered
- 1 medium zucchini, cut into 1/2-inch (1 cm) slices
- 16 medium mushrooms

MARINADE

- 1/4 cup (50 mL) freshly squeezed lime juice
- 2 Tbsp (30 mL) freshly squeezed lemon juice
- 2 Tbsp (30 mL) dry white wine
- 1 Tbsp (15 mL) olive oil
- 1 small onion, finely chopped
- 2 large cloves garlic, peeled and crushed
- 1/4 cup (50 mL) finely chopped cilantro
- 2 tsp (10 mL) grated fresh ginger
- Salt and freshly ground pepper to taste

- Cut tuna into about 1 1/2-inch (4 cm) cubes. In a bowl, whisk together all the marinade ingredients. Add tuna and toss well to coat. Cover with plastic wrap and marinate in refrigerator 2 hours. Add vegetables and marinate 5 minutes more.

- Preheat broiler.

- Thread marinated vegetables onto metal skewers, alternating with tuna. Place in a shallow baking dish, and broil about 15 minutes or until fish is opaque and flakes easily when tested with a fork.

POACHED FISH

SERVES 2

INGREDIENTS

- 6 cups (1.5 L) water
- 2/3 cup (150 mL) red wine vinegar
- 2 large cloves garlic, peeled and quartered
- 1 celery stick, roughly chopped
- 1 small onion, quartered
- 1 Tbsp (15 mL) finely chopped fresh parsley
- 1 Tbsp (15 mL) finely chopped fresh chives
- 1/2 tsp (2 mL) celery salt
- 1/2 tsp (2 mL) dried Herbes de Provence
- 1 bay leaf
- Pinch freshly ground black pepper
- Salt and pepper
- 4 fillets of cod or turbot

- In a saucepan, bring water to a boil. Add all ingredients except salt, pepper and fish, cover, and simmer 30 minutes.

- Strain the stock through a fine-mesh sieve, and return to saucepan. Bring back to a boil, then turn heat down. Season fish fillets with salt and pepper, and poach in simmering stock 5 minutes, or until fillets are opaque and flake easily when tested with a fork.

- *Serving suggestion:* Serve with peppers, red & yellow pepper medley (p. 174) or pink sauce with red peppers (p. 80).

SALMON STEAKS

SERVES 4

INGREDIENTS

- 1/2 cup (125 mL) dry white wine
- 1/4 cup (50 mL) freshly squeezed lemon juice
- 2 tsp (10 mL) olive oil
- 2 large cloves garlic, peeled and crushed
- 1 Tbsp (15 mL) finely chopped fresh parsley
- 1/2 tsp (2 mL) dried tarragon
- Salt and pepper to taste
- 4 salmon steaks

- In a large bowl, mix all ingredients except salmon. Add salmon steaks, turning over to coat well. Marinate in refrigerator about 1 hour.

- Preheat broiler.

- Arrange salmon steaks in an ovenproof dish, and broil about 5 minutes on each side, or until fish is opaque and flakes easily when tested with a fork.

SALMON TIDBITS

INGREDIENTS

- 1/2 lb (225 g) cooked salmon
- 1/4 cup (50 mL) chopped celery
- 2 green onions, finely sliced
- 1 large egg, beaten
- 1 Tbsp (15 mL) freshly grated Romano cheese
- 1 Tbsp (15 mL) oat bran
- 3 Tbsp (45 mL) finely chopped fresh parsley
- 1 Tbsp (15 mL) finely chopped fresh dill
- 1/4 tsp (1 mL) celery salt
- Freshly ground black pepper to taste
- 1 Tbsp (15 mL) olive oil

- In a large bowl, combine cooked salmon, celery, onions, egg, cheese, bran and seasonings. Shape into 12 portions.

- In a large nonstick skillet, over medium heat, heat olive oil, and cook salmon portions 3 to 4 minutes on either side, or until hot and golden.

- *Variation:* Use tuna instead of salmon.

SCALLOP GRATIN

SERVES 3 TO 4

INGREDIENTS

- 1/3 cup (75 mL) freshly squeezed lime juice
- 1 Tbsp (15 mL) olive oil
- 1/4 cup (50 mL) finely chopped red pepper
- 1/4 cup (50 mL) finely chopped fresh parsley
- 1/4 cup (50 mL) finely chopped fresh chives
- Salt and freshly ground pepper to taste
- 1 1/2 lb (675 g) fresh medium-size scallops
- 3 1/2 oz (100 g) Bocconcini cheese, thinly sliced

- In a bowl, beat together lime juice, olive oil, red pepper and seasonings. Add scallops and stir well to cover. Marinate in refrigerator 1 hour.

- Preheat broiler.

- Divide scallops between 4 individual gratin dishes. Top with Bocconcini slices, pour marinade over and bake 8 to 10 minutes, or until scallops turn opaque.

SEAFOOD BROCHETTES

SERVES 4

INGREDIENTS

- 12 large shrimp, shelled and deveined
- 12 large scallops
- 12 small onions, peeled
- 12 cherry tomatoes
- 1 green pepper, cut into large pieces

MARINADE

- 3/4 cup (175 mL) olive oil
- 2 Tbsp (30 mL) freshly squeezed lemon juice
- 1 Tbsp (15 mL) freshly squeezed lime juice
- 1 large clove garlic, peeled and crushed
- Salt and pepper to taste
- 2 Tbsp (30 mL) grated fresh ginger
- 1 Tbsp (15 mL) finely chopped fresh dill

- In a bowl, mix marinade ingredients, reserving 1/4 for basting. Put shrimp and scallops in marinade and refrigerate about 45 minutes.

- Boil onions in lightly salted water until tender.

- Preheat oven to 450°F (230°C).

- Thread marinated shrimp and scallops onto metal skewers, alternating with vegetables. Baste onions, tomatoes and pepper with rest of marinade.

- Bake about 10 minutes turning over and basting midway through cooking.

SHRIMP & SCALLOPS WITH LEEKS

SERVES 4

INGREDIENTS

- 2 Tbsp (30 mL) olive oil
- 3 large leeks, white parts only, sliced
- 1 cup (250 mL) homemade defatted chicken stock (see p. 78)
- 2 Tbsp (30 mL) finely chopped fresh dill
- 1/2 tsp (2 mL) curry powder
- 1/4 tsp (1 mL) fennel seeds
- Pinch cayenne pepper
- Salt and pepper to taste
- 1/2 lb (225 g) medium, fresh shrimp, peeled and deveined
- 1/2 lb (225 g) medium, fresh scallops
- 1 Tbsp freshly squeezed lemon juice
- 1 tsp (5 mL) tamari sauce
- 1/2 tsp (2 mL) onion powder

- In a large nonstick skillet, over medium heat, heat oil and cook leeks 5 minutes. Add half the chicken stock, dill, curry, fennel seeds and cayenne. Cook 3 to 4 minutes more. Season with salt and pepper.

- Add shrimp, scallops, lemon juice, tamari, onion powder and rest of stock. Stir well, cover and cook over medium heat 5 minutes, or until scallops are opaque and shrimp turn pink. Stir occasionally, adding a little chicken stock, if necessary, to prevent drying.

SOLE EN PAPILLOTE

SERVES 4

INGREDIENTS

- 2 Tbsp (30 mL) olive oil
- 1 small red onion, finely chopped
- 1/2 yellow pepper, cut into strips
- 2 Tbsp (30 mL) pesto sauce
- 1/2 cup (125 mL) dry white wine
- 4 medium ripe tomatoes, peeled and roughly chopped
- 8 black olives, pitted and thinly sliced
- 1 Tbsp (15 mL) capers
- 1 small clove garlic, peeled and crushed
- Salt and freshly ground pepper to taste
- 4 sole fillets
- 2 Tbsp (30 mL) freshly squeezed lime juice

- In a skillet, over medium heat, heat olive oil, add onion, pepper and pesto, and cook 5 minutes. Add wine and bring to boil. Reduce heat and simmer 3 to 4 minutes or until liquid has evaporated.

- Add tomatoes, olives and capers, and continue cooking 5 minutes more or until sauce has thickened. Season with salt and pepper.

- Preheat oven to 425°F (220°C).

- Wipe fillets with a paper towel, and place each one on a separate sheet of aluminum foil about 15 inches (40 cm) long. Cover with sauce and sprinkle lime juice over. Fold aluminum foil over fillets, turn edges in and pinch to seal.

- Bake about 15 minutes, or until fish is opaque and flakes easily when tested with a fork.

- *Note:* To peel tomatoes, plunge into boiling water 30 seconds; skin will slide off easily.

SPICY SHRIMP WITH GINGER

SERVES 3 TO 4

INGREDIENTS

- 1 lb (450 g) large fresh shrimp, shelled and deveined
- 1/2 tsp (2 mL) paprika
- 1/2 tsp (2 mL) Cajun seasoning
- 1/4 tsp (1 mL) chili powder
- 1/8 tsp (0.5 mL) cayenne pepper
- Pinch onion powder
- 1 Tbsp (15 mL) olive oil
- 1 large clove garlic, peeled and crushed
- 1 Tbsp (15 mL) grated fresh ginger
- Juice of 1 fresh lime

- In a bowl, combine seasonings. Add shrimp and stir to coat.

- In a skillet, over medium-high heat, heat oil and cook shrimp 2 minutes. Add garlic and ginger. Season with salt and pepper; and add lime juice. Cook 1 to 2 minutes more, or until shrimp turn pink.

STUFFED RAINBOW TROUT

SERVES 4

INGREDIENTS

- 4 rainbow or grey whole trout, cleaned
- Olive oil
- 1 lime, sliced

STUFFING

- 1 Tbsp (15 mL) olive oil
- 1/2 fresh fennel bulb
- 1/2 cup (125 mL) chopped mushrooms
- 1/2 cup (125 mL) chopped red pepper
- 2 Tbsp (30 mL) thinly sliced green onion
- 2 Tbsp (30 mL) freshly squeezed lime juice
- 2 Tbsp (30 mL) finely chopped fresh parsley
- Salt and pepper to taste

- *To make stuffing:* In a skillet, over low heat, heat olive oil, add fennel, mushrooms, red pepper and onion, and cook 5 minutes. Add lime juice and seasonings, and continue cooking 1 minute.

- Preheat oven to 400°F (200°C).

- Rinse fish under running cold water inside and out, and wipe dry. Stuff cavity with fennel mixture.

- Using olive oil, grease 4 rectangular pieces of aluminum foil. Place 1 trout on each, cover with lime slices, and seal. Transfer to a baking dish and bake 15 minutes, or until fish turns opaque and flakes easily when tested with a fork.

TROUT SURPRISE

SERVES 4

INGREDIENTS

- 1/2 cup (125 mL) sour cream
- 1/4 cup (50 mL) plain yogurt
- 1 Tbsp (30 mL) finely chopped red onion
- 1 Tbsp (30 mL) finely chopped fresh chives
- 1 tsp (5 mL) finely chopped fresh dill
- Olive oil
- 4 trout fillets
- Freshly ground black pepper to taste

- Preheat oven to 425°F (220°C).

- In a mixing bowl, combine sour cream, yogurt, onion and herbs.

- Arrange fillets in a lightly oiled ovenproof dish, season with pepper and cover with sour cream sauce.

- Bake uncovered 12 minutes. Cover with aluminum foil and bake 5 minutes more, or until fish is opaque and flakes easily when tested with a fork.

TURBOT FILLETS STUFFED WITH SHRIMP

SERVES 4

INGREDIENTS

- 1/4 lb (100 g) peeled and deveined shrimp
- 2 Tbsp (30 mL) plain yogurt
- 1 large egg white
- 1 tsp (5 mL) finely chopped fresh chives
- 1/2 tsp (2 mL) paprika
- A few spinach leaves, washed and trimmed
- 4 turbot fillets
- 1/4 cup (50 mL) dry white wine
- 1 Tbsp (15 mL) freshly squeezed lemon juice
- Salt and pepper to taste

SAUCE

- 1 tsp (5 mL) olive oil
- 1 green onion, thinly sliced
- 3/4 cup (175 mL) homemade defatted chicken stock (see p. 78)
- Pinch saffron powder
- Pinch curry powder
- Pinch onion powder
- Salt and pepper to taste
- 3 Tbsp (45 mL) 15% m.f. cream

- In a blender or food processor, purée shrimp while gradually adding yogurt. Transfer to a bowl and reserve.

- In another bowl, beat egg white until soft peaks are formed and, with a spatula, fold into shrimp mixture. Add chives and paprika; mix and reserve.

- Steam spinach 30 to 60 seconds until wilted, and reserve.

- Preheat oven to 400°F (200°C).

- In a baking dish, place 2 fillets, cover each with spinach leaf and spoon shrimp mixture over. Place remaining 2 fillets on top. Pour wine and lemon juice over, season with salt and pepper. Bake, covered, 10 to 15 minutes, or until fish is opaque and flakes easily when tested with a fork.

- Meanwhile, in a saucepan, over high heat, heat olive oil and sautée green onion. Add stock and seasonings, lower heat and simmer 2 minutes. Stir in cream, and, over medium heat, continue cooking 5 minutes, stirring occasionally, until mixture thickens. Spoon sauce over fillets.

EGGS

BROCCOLI OMELETTE

SERVES 4

INGREDIENTS

- 2 Tbsp (30 mL) olive oil
- 1/3 head of broccoli, separated into florets
- 3 green onions, finely sliced
- 1 medium tomato, deseeded and diced
- 1 large clove garlic, peeled and crushed
- 6 large eggs
- 1/4 cup (50 mL) milk
- Salt and pepper to taste
- 2 Tbsp (30 mL) finely chopped fresh parsley
- 1/2 cup (125 mL) grated partly skimmed cheddar cheese
- 1/4 cup (50 mL) freshly grated Parmesan cheese

- In an ovenproof skillet, over low heat, heat olive oil and cook broccoli, green onions, tomato and garlic 5 minutes.

- Meanwhile, in a bowl, beat eggs and milk. Season with salt and pepper, and add parsley.

- Preheat broiler.

- Pour egg mixture over vegetables, stir quickly and cook about 5 minutes. Cover with cheeses, transfer to broiler to finish cooking and serve immediately.

MEXICAN OMELETTE

SERVES 4

INGREDIENTS

- 5 large eggs
- 1/2 cup (125 mL) milk
- 1-2 tsp (5-10 mL) chili powder
- Salt and pepper
- 1 Tbsp (15 mL) olive oil
- 1/2 cup (125 mL) thinly sliced mushrooms
- 1/2 red pepper, diced
- 1 small tomato, diced
- 1 green onions, thinly sliced
- 1 small clove garlic, peeled and crushed
- 3/4 cup (175 mL) grated sharp cheddar cheese

- In a mixing bowl, beat eggs with milk and chili powder. Season with salt and pepper to taste, and set aside.

- In a ovenproof skillet, heat olive oil, and cook the vegetables and garlic over low heat for a few minutes, or until mushrooms are tender.

- Preheat broiler.

- Pour egg mixture over the vegetables, stir very quickly and cook about 5 minutes more. Cover with grated cheddar and broil until cheese has melted.

MUSHROOM OMELETTE SOUFFLÉ

SERVES 4

INGREDIENTS

- Olive oil
- 2 cups (500 mL) sliced mushrooms
- 2 green onions, thinly sliced
- 1 large clove garlic, peeled and crushed
- 4 large egg yolks
- 1/3 cup (75 mL) milk
- 2 Tbsp (30 mL) finely chopped fresh parsley
- 4 large egg whites
- Salt and pepper to taste

- In a nonstick skillet, over medium heat, heat 2 Tbsp olive oil. Add mushrooms, green onions and garlic, and cook 5 minutes. Transfer to a plate, and reserve.

- In a bowl, beat egg yolks together with milk and parsley. Reserve.

- In another bowl, beat egg whites until soft peaks form. Using a spatula, gently fold egg whites into egg yolk mixture.

- In the same skillet, over medium heat, heat 1 Tbsp olive oil. Pour in eggs, and cook 1 minute, or until eggs start to set. Cover with mushroom mixture. Season with salt and pepper, and cook 1 minute longer.

- Using a spatula, fold omelette in two, and slide onto a serving dish.

RED PEPPER & BLACK OLIVE FRITTATA

SERVES 4

INGREDIENTS

- 1 Tbsp (15 mL) olive oil
- 1 medium red pepper, cut into strips
- 2 green onions, thinly sliced
- 1 clove garlic, peeled and crushed
- Pinch celery salt
- Pinch onion powder
- 4 large eggs
- 4 large egg whites
- 3 Tbsp (45 mL) finely chopped fresh parsley
- 2 Tbsp (30 mL) finely chopped fresh chives
- 1/4 tsp (1 mL) dried basil
- Fresh ground black pepper to taste
- 1/2 cup (125 mL) 5% m.f. ricotta cheese
- 1/4 cup (50 mL) freshly grated Romano or Parmesan cheese
- 5 black olives, pitted and thinly sliced

- In a large, nonstick, ovenproof skillet, over medium heat, heat 2 tsp of the oil. Add pepper and onions, and cook 10 minutes, or until pepper is tender. Add garlic, and cook 30 seconds, stirring constantly. Remove from skillet and let cool about 10 minutes.

- In a bowl, whisk whole eggs with egg whites. Add all the seasonings, along with cheeses. Mix well until mixture is smooth, and fold in vegetables.

- Preheat broiler, remove top shelf to make sure there is a space of 6 inches (15 cm) between heating element and skillet.

- In the same skillet, over medium-low heat, heat rest of olive oil. Pour in egg mixture, making sure skillet is evenly filled. Garnish with olives and cook 5 to 6 minutes, or until set around the edges and golden. Finish cooking under broiler 2 minutes, or until top is set and golden. Serve immediately.

SCRAMBLED EGGS & HAM

SERVES 4

INGREDIENTS

- 1 Tbsp (15 mL) olive oil
- 2/3 cup (150 mL) diced ham
- 1 green onion, finely chopped
- 1/4 red pepper, diced
- 1 clove garlic, peeled and crushed
- 8 medium eggs
- 1/2 cup (125 mL) milk
- Salt and pepper to taste
- 1 Tbsp (15 mL) finely chopped fresh parsley

- In a nonstick pan, over low heat, heat oil. Add ham and cook until golden. Add onion, red pepper, garlic and cook 30 seconds.

- In a bowl, beat eggs and milk, and pour mixture over the ham. Season with salt and pepper; add parsley, and cook over medium heat. As soon as the eggs start setting, break up with a spatula, stirring occasionally until eggs are thick and creamy.

TOMATOES STUFFED
WITH EGGS

SERVES 4

INGREDIENTS

- 8 medium tomatoes
- 8 medium eggs
- 1/2 cup (125 mL) milk
- Salt and pepper to taste
- 1 Tbsp (15 mL) olive oil
- 4 green onions, finely sliced
- 1/2 green pepper, diced
- 1 large clove garlic, peeled and crushed
- 2 tsp (10 mL) finely chopped fresh chives
- 2 tsp (10 mL) finely chopped fresh basil

- Preheat oven to 375°F (190°C).

- Cut tops off tomatoes and scoop out flesh with a spoon. Lightly salt inside of tomatoes and turn upside down on paper towels to drain, about 10 minutes.

- Place tomatoes in ovenproof dish and bake 10 minutes. Remove and keep warm.

- In a bowl, beat eggs and milk. Season with salt and pepper. Set aside.

- In a large skillet, over low heat, heat olive oil and cook the remaining ingredients until vegetables are tender. Pour egg mixture over, and cook over medium heat until eggs begin to set, then break up with a spatula to scramble. Stir occasionally until eggs are thick and creamy.

- Fill tomatoes with egg mixture, and serve.

VEGETABLE
SIDE DISHES

BRUSSELS SPROUTS

SERVES 4

INGREDIENTS

- 7 oz (200 g) Brussels sprouts
- 2 Tbsp (30 mL) olive oil
- 1/2 small red or yellow onion, thinly sliced
- Salt and pepper to taste
- Pinch nutmeg
- 1 Tbsp (15 mL) freshly squeezed lime juice
- 3 Tbsp (45 mL) finely chopped fresh parsley

- Cut stems and discard outer leaves of sprouts. Rinse under running water. Score base of each sprout in a crisscross direction, and steam 15 minutes.

- In a skillet, over low heat, heat olive oil, and cook sprouts and onion until tender. Season with salt, pepper and nutmeg. Add lime juice and parsley, and stir. Serve immediately.

CAULIFLOWER & ZUCCHINI CURRY

SERVES 4

INGREDIENTS

- 1 Tbsp (15 mL) olive oil
- 1 large onion, chopped
- 1 large clove garlic, peeled and crushed
- 2 tsp (10 mL) curry powder
- 1 small head cauliflower cut into florets
- 1 small zucchini, thinly sliced
- 1 tsp (5 mL) tomato paste
- 1/2 cup (125 mL) homemade defatted chicken stock (see p. 78)
- 1/2 cup (125 mL) plain yogurt
- 2 tsp (10 mL) finely chopped fresh parsley

- In a saucepan, over low heat, heat olive oil, add onion and cook until onion is tender. Add garlic and curry powder, and cook 2 minutes more.

- Add cauliflower, zucchini, tomato paste and stock. Stir well, cover and simmer 8 to 10 minutes, or until vegetables are crisp-tender.

- Add yogurt and parsley; stir, and serve.

CRISP VEGETABLES WITH SOUR CREAM

SERVES 4

INGREDIENTS

- 2 Tbsp (30 mL) olive oil
- 1/2 medium onion, coarsely chopped
- 1/2 medium zucchini, thinly sliced
- 1/3 head broccoli, separated into florets
- 1/3 medium cauliflower, separated into florets
- 1/2 red pepper, cut into strips
- 1 large clove garlic, peeled and crushed
- 1/4 cup (50 mL) homemade defatted chicken stock (see p. 78)
- 1/2 tsp (2 mL) coriander powder
- 1/2 tsp (2 mL) turmeric powder
- 1/2 tsp (2 mL) ginger powder
- Salt and pepper to taste
- 1/4 cup (50 mL) plain yogurt
- 1/4 cup (50 mL) sour cream
- 1 Tbsp (15 mL) finely chopped fresh parsley

- In a saucepan, over low heat, heat olive oil and cook vegetables 7 to 8 minutes.

- Add garlic, chicken stock and seasonings. Simmer 3 minutes or until vegetables are crisp-tender.

- Stir in yogurt, sour cream and parsley. Mix well and serve.

EGGPLANT & TOMATO GRATIN

SERVES 4

INGREDIENTS

- 8 slices eggplant, cut across the width to about 1/2-inch (1 cm) thickness
- Olive oil
- 8 slices ripe tomato
- 2 Tbsp (30 mL) pesto sauce
- Salt and pepper to taste
- 1/3 lb (150 g) Bocconcini (fresh mozzarella), sliced
- Wheat bran

- Steam eggplant 3 minutes, and drain on paper towels.

- Preheat broiler.

- In a lightly oiled ovenproof dish, arrange eggplant slices in a layer, top with tomato slices and season with pesto, salt and pepper. Cover with cheese slices, dust generously with bran, and broil about 4 minutes.

GREEN PEAS &
PEARL ONIONS

SERVES 4

INGREDIENTS

- 10 pearl onions, peeled
- 2 Tbsp (30 mL) olive oil
- 1 large clove garlic, peeled and crushed
- 3/4 lb (350 g) frozen peas, defrosted
- 1 1/2 Tbsp (22 mL) tamari sauce
- 1 1/2 Tbsp (22 mL) freshly squeezed lime juice
- 1/4 tsp (1 mL) balsamic vinegar
- 1/2 tsp (2 mL) dried thyme
- Salt and pepper to taste

- Boil onions in lightly salted water until tender.

- In a saucepan, over low heat, heat olive oil, add onions and garlic and cook 3 minutes.

- Add peas and rest of ingredients. Stir well, cover and cook over medium heat 7 to 8 minutes, stirring occasionally.

GRILLED ZUCCHINI

SERVES 4

INGREDIENTS

- 2 Tbsp (30 mL) olive oil
- 2 Tbsp (30 mL) freshly squeezed lime juice
- 2 tsp (10 mL) tamari sauce
- 2 cloves garlic, peeled and crushed
- 1/2 Tbsp (7 mL) pesto sauce
- Salt and pepper to taste
- 2 medium zucchini, cut in half lengthwise

- Whisk together marinade ingredients. Baste zucchini slices generously with marinade, and transfer to a hot skillet. Cook over low heat about 5 minutes on each side, or until zucchini are tender. Baste as needed during the cooking. For a more grilled effect, cook over medium heat another 1 to 2 minutes.

LEEKS IN CREAM

SERVES 2 TO 3

INGREDIENTS

- 1 1/2 Tbsp (22 mL) olive oil
- 2 large leeks, white part only, thinly sliced
- 1/2 cup (125 mL) homemade defatted chicken stock (see p. 78)
- 1 Tbsp (15 mL) freshly squeezed lime juice
- 2 Tbsp (30 mL) finely chopped fresh parsley
- 1/4 tsp (1 mL) curry powder
- 1/4 tsp (1 mL) celery salt
- 1/4 tsp (1 mL) onion salt
- Pinch ground black pepper
- 2 Tbsp (30 mL) 15% m.f. cream

- In a nonstick skillet, over low heat, heat olive oil, add leeks and cook about 12 minutes.

- Add stock, lime juice and seasonings. Stir well, and cook 10 minutes more.

- Add cream and continue to cook over low heat 5 minutes, or until leeks are soft. Stir occasionally and, if necessary, add a little more chicken stock.

RATATOUILLE

SERVES 4

INGREDIENTS

- 2 Tbsp (30 mL) olive oil
- 10 small onions, peeled
- 1 1/2 cups (375 mL) crushed tomatoes
- 1/4 cup (50 mL) tomato juice
- 1 medium egg plant, chopped
- 1 medium zucchini, chopped
- 1/2 green pepper, chopped
- 1/2 red pepper, chopped
- 1/2 cup (125 mL) green beans, cut in half
- 1/2 cup (125 mL) wax beans, cut in half
- 1 large clove garlic, peeled and crushed
- 2 Tbsp (30 mL) pesto sauce
- 1 Tbsp (15 mL) tamari sauce
- 1 tsp (5 mL) dried Herbes de Provence
- 1/2 tsp (2 mL) dried thyme
- Salt and pepper to taste

- Heat olive oil in a saucepan over low heat, add onions and cook 2 minutes.

- Add rest of the ingredients, cover and simmer 20 minutes or until vegetables are crisp-tender.

RED & YELLOW PEPPER MEDLEY

SERVES 4

INGREDIENTS

- 1/4 cup (50 mL) olive oil
- 2 medium red peppers, cut into thin strips
- 2 medium yellow peppers, cut into thin strips
- 1 small clove garlic, peeled and crushed
- 2 Tbsp (30 mL) tamari sauce
- 1 Tbsp (15 mL) freshly squeezed lime juice
- 1/4 tsp (1 mL) dried Herbes de Provence
- 1/4 tsp (1 mL) curry powder
- Pinch onion powder
- Pepper to taste

- In a large pan, over medium heat, heat olive oil. Add peppers and cook 5 minutes.

- Add rest of the ingredients and mix well. Cover and continue cooking until vegetables are tender, stirring occasionally.

LEGUMES
&
GRAINS

BEAN & CHICKPEA SALAD

SERVES 4

INGREDIENTS

- 1 celery stick, diced
- 1/2 green pepper, diced
- 1/2 red pepper, diced
- 2 green onions, finely sliced
- 1 cup (250 mL) cooked red beans
  (see cooking method, p. 220)
- 1 cup (250 mL) cooked chickpeas
  (see cooking method, p. 220)
- 1/4 cup (50 mL) fresh parsley, finely chopped
- Balsamic vinaigrette (see p. 59)

- In a salad bowl, toss vegetables. Dress with vinaigrette and toss to coat ingredients well. Let sit 15 minutes before serving.

BROWN BASMATI
RICE & BLACK BEANS

SERVES 4

INGREDIENTS

- 2 cups (500 mL) homemade defatted chicken stock (see p. 78)
- 1 cup (250 mL) brown basmati rice
- 1 tsp (5 mL) olive oil
- 1/2 small zucchini, diced
- 1/4 red pepper, diced
- 1/4 yellow pepper, diced
- 1 clove garlic, peeled and crushed
- 3/4 cup (175 mL) homemade (see p. 78) or commercial unsweetened salsa
- 2 cups (500 mL) cooked black beans (see cooking method, p. 220)
- 1 cup (250 mL) 5% m.f. sour cream
- 3 Tbsp (45 mL) finely chopped fresh parsley

- In a saucepan, bring chicken stock to boil. Rinse and drain rice, and add to stock. Cover and simmer 40 minutes, or until rice has absorbed the stock and is tender.

- Meanwhile, in another pan, over medium heat, heat oil and cook zucchini, peppers and garlic 5 minutes. Add salsa and black beans, and stir well. Cook 3 minutes longer. Remove from heat and let stand in a warm place.

- *To serve:* Divide rice evenly among 4 plates, spoon bean mixture on top, add a dollop of sour cream to each serving and garnish with parsley.

CHEESE & SPINACH ROLLS

SERVES 4

INGREDIENTS

- 4 wholewheat lasagna sheets
- 4 wholewheat spinach lasagna sheets
- 1 Tbsp (15 mL) olive oil
- 1/2 medium onion, finely chopped
- 6 mushrooms, thinly sliced
- 1/3 celery stick, thinly sliced
- 3 1/4 cups (800 mL) crushed tomatoes
- 2 cloves garlic, peeled and crushed
- 1/2 Tbsp (7 mL) dried thyme
- 1/2 tsp (2 mL) dried savory
- Salt and pepper to taste

GARNISH

- 1 medium fresh egg, beaten
- 3 medium hard-cooked eggs
- 3/4 cup (175 mL) cottage cheese
- 1/2 cup (125 mL) grated part-skimmed mozzarella or cheddar cheese
- 1/2 cup (125 mL) freshly grated Parmesan cheese
- 1 Tbsp (30 mL) finely chopped fresh parsley
- 1 cup (250 mL) steamed, well-drained spinach

- Cook lasagna in boiling water for 12 minutes.

- Meanwhile, in a saucepan over low heat, heat olive oil and cook onions, mushrooms and celery until tender. Add tomatoes, garlic and seasonings. Stir well, cover and let simmer 10 minutes.

- Preheat oven to 350°F (180°C).

- Rinse lasagna in cold water and pat dry with paper towel. In a bowl, combine first 6 ingredients of garnish, and spread mixture on lasagna. Place spinach on top and roll.

- Cover bottom of an ovenproof dish with tomato mixture. Place lasagna rolls in dish and pour rest of tomato sauce over. Bake 30 to 35 minutes. Let sit 5 minutes before serving.

HERBED LENTILS
& TOMATOES

SERVES 4

INGREDIENTS

- 4 cups (1 L) cooked green lentils
  (see cooking method, p. 220)
- Juice of 1 lemon
- 1 Tbsp (15 mL) olive oil
- 1 medium onion, finely sliced
- 2 celery sticks, finely sliced
- 1 clove garlic, peeled and crushed
- 1 Tbsp (15 mL) finely chopped fresh parsley
- 1 tsp (5 mL) dried Herbes de Provence
- Salt and freshly ground black pepper to taste
- 6 very ripe tomatoes, cut into quarters and deseeded

- Place cooked lentils in a serving bowl, and set aside.

- In a nonstick skillet, over low heat, heat olive oil, add onion, celery, garlic, parsley and herbs, and cook about 4 to 5 minutes. Season with salt and pepper, and add mixture to lentils. Mix well.

- Preheat oven to 300°F (150°C).

- Add tomatoes to lentil mixture, transfer to a baking dish and bake 15 to 20 minutes.

- *Note:* To peel tomatoes, place in boiling water 30 seconds; skin will peel off easily.

LEMON DILL LENTIL & CHICKPEA SALAD

SERVES 4

INGREDIENTS

- 1 1/4 cups (300 mL) cooked green lentils (see cooking method, p. 220)
- 1 1/4 cups (300 mL) cooked chickpeas (see cooking method, p. 220)
- 10 cherry tomatoes
- 1 medium zucchini, diced
- 1/2 yellow or orange pepper, diced
- 1/3 cup (75 mL) finely chopped fresh chives

VINAIGRETTE

- 1/4 cup (50 mL) extra-virgin olive oil
- 2 Tbsp (30 mL) freshly squeezed lemon juice
- 1/3 cup (75 mL) finely chopped fresh dill
- Salt and freshly ground black pepper to taste

- In a salad bowl, mix together lentils, chickpeas and vegetables.
- In a bowl, whisk together vinaigrette ingredients. Pour over salad and stir to coat well. Let stand 30 minutes at room temperature before serving.

MEDITERRANEAN STEW

SERVES 4

INGREDIENTS

- 1 medium red pepper, roughly chopped
- 1/2 medium green pepper, roughly chopped
- 1 bulb fennel, roughly chopped
- 1/2 small cauliflower, cut into florets
- 1 medium zucchini, cut into 1/2-inch (1 cm) slices
- 2 medium onions, chopped
- 2 cups (500 mL) crushed tomatoes
- 1/3 cup (75 mL) tomato paste
- 1 cup (250 mL) homemade defatted chicken stock (see p. 78)
- 2 large cloves garlic, peeled and crushed
- 1/2 jalapeño or similar hot pepper, finely chopped
- 1 Tbsp (15 mL) olive oil
- 2 bay leaves
- 2 Tbsp (30 mL) finely chopped fresh parsley
- 1 tsp (5 mL) dried thyme
- 1/2 tsp (2 mL) paprika
- 1/4 tsp (1 mL) celery salt
- Pinch turmeric
- Salt and freshly ground black pepper to taste
- 1/2 lb (225 g) firm tofu, diced
- 1 1/2 cups (375 mL) cooked green lentils (see cooking method, p. 220)

- In a large saucepan, combine all ingredients except tofu and lentils. Mix well, and simmer 20 minutes.

- Add tofu and lentils, and cook about 10 minutes more, or until vegetables are crisp-tender, stirring occasionally.

MILLET & VEGETABLE SALAD

SERVES 4

INGREDIENTS

- 2 cups (500 mL) water
- 1/2 tsp (2 mL) concentrated vegetable stock
- 1 cup (250 mL) millet, rinsed in lukewarm water
- 1 large very ripe tomato, diced
- 1/2 green pepper, diced
- 1/2 red pepper, diced
- 1/4 zucchini, diced
- 1 small clove garlic, peeled and crushed
- 1/4 cup (50 mL) freshly squeezed lime juice
- 2 Tbsp (30 mL) pitted and thinly sliced green olives
- 1 Tbsp (15 mL) capers
- 1 tsp (5 mL) pesto sauce
- 2 Tbsp (30 mL) finely chopped fresh parsley
- 3 Tbsp (45 mL) finely chopped fresh chives
- Pinch curry powder
- Salt and pepper to taste

- In a saucepan, bring the water and stock to boil and add millet. Cover and simmer 20 to 25 minutes. Remove from stove and let sit, covered, 10 minutes.

- Drain millet, place in a salad bowl and refrigerate 1 to 1 1/2 hours.

- Fluff millet with a fork and add the remaining ingredients. Mix well and refrigerate 1 hour before serving.

PASTA SALAD

SERVES 2 TO 3

INGREDIENTS

- 1 1/2 cups (375 mL) wholewheat fusilli pasta shells
- 2 Tbsp (30 mL) olive oil
- 1 small zucchini, diced
- 1/2 red pepper, diced
- 1/2 yellow pepper, diced
- 1/2 green pepper, diced
- 2 green onions, thinly sliced
- 2 tsp (10 mL) freshly squeezed lime juice
- 15 cherry tomatoes, quartered
- 1 large clove garlic, peeled and crushed
- 2 Tbsp (30 mL) finely chopped fresh parsley
- 1 Tbsp (15 mL) finely chopped fresh basil
- Pinch chili powder
- Pinch celery salt
- Pinch onion salt
- Salt and pepper to taste

- Cook pasta in boiling salted water 10 minutes; drain.

- In a skillet, over high heat, heat olive oil, and sauté zucchini, peppers and green onions 2 minutes. Add lime juice and cook 1 to 2 minutes more, or until vegetables are crisp-tender. Transfer to a salad bowl, add rest of ingredients and pasta, and toss. Cover and refrigerate 2 hours.

- Serve cold or at room temperature.

RICE & LENTILS

SERVES 4

INGREDIENTS

- 1 1/2 cups (375 mL) cooked green lentils
  (see cooking method, p. 220)
- 1 1/2 cups (375 mL) cooked brown basmati rice
  (see cooking method, p. 220)
- 1 small onion, finely chopped
- 1 large clove garlic, peeled and crushed
- 1/4 cup (50 mL) finely chopped fresh parsley

DRESSING

- 1/4 cup (50 mL) extra-virgin olive oil
- 2 Tbsp (30 mL) freshly squeezed lemon juice
- 1 1/2 Tbsp (22 mL) tamari sauce
- 1/2-1 Tbsp (7-15 mL) pesto
- Salt and pepper to taste

- In a bowl, combine all ingredients. Mix thoroughly and refrigerate 30 minutes before serving.

SPICY LASAGNA

SERVES 4

INGREDIENTS

- 12 sheets wholewheat lasagna
- 1 Tbsp (15 mL) olive oil
- 1 small onion, finely chopped
- 2 cups (500 mL) chopped tomatoes
- 2 cups (500 mL) tomato sauce
- 1/4 cup (50 mL) tomato paste
- 1 large clove garlic, peeled and crushed
- 1 tsp (5 mL) dried basil
- 1 tsp (5 mL) dried oregano
- 2 cups (500 mL) 5% m.f. ricotta cheese
- 2 cups (500 mL) 2% m.f. cottage cheese
- 1 cup (250 mL) cooked black beans
  (for cooking method, see p. 220)
- 1 cup (250 mL) steamed, drained spinach
- 1 cup (250 mL) homemade (see p. 78) or commercial
  unsweetened salsa
- 1 1/2 (375 mL) grated hard cheese

- Cook lasagna in boiling salted water 12 minutes, and drain.

- Meanwhile, in a saucepan, over low heat, heat olive oil, add onion and cook until tender. Add tomatoes, tomato sauce and paste, garlic and seasonings. Stir well, partially cover, and simmer 10 minutes.

- Preheat oven to 350°F (180°C).

- In a bowl, combine ricotta and cottage cheese. Add beans and spinach, and mix. Reserve.

- In a baking dish to fit lasagna, place 3 strips, cover well with tomato sauce, and top with ricotta mixture. Repeat for a second layer.

- Cover third layer of lasagna with salsa and tomato sauce, making sure pasta is well covered. Top with rest of ricotta mixture. Place a final layer of lasagna on top, cover well with tomato sauce, sprinkle grated cheese on top, and bake 35 minutes.

STUFFED EGGPLANT

SERVES 4

INGREDIENTS

- 2 medium eggplants
- 2 cups (500 mL) diced tomatoes
- 2 cups (500 mL) cooked green lentils (see cooking method, p. 220)
- 1/2 tsp (2 mL) tamari sauce
- 1 tsp (5 mL) dried Herbes de Provence
- Salt and freshly ground pepper to taste
- 1 1/2 cups (375 mL) grated Swiss cheese (Gruyère or Emmenthal)

- Preheat oven to 375°F (190°C).

- Cut eggplant in half, lengthwise, and scoop out pulp, leaving about 1/2-inch (1 cm) thickness. Wrap in aluminum foil and bake 30 minutes.

- Preheat oven to 475°F (240°C).

- In a bowl, place tomatoes, lentils, tamari and seasonings, and mix well. Stuff eggplant halves with this mixture, and cover with grated cheese. Place eggplants in a baking dish and bake 10 to 12 minutes, or until cheese has melted and is golden. Serve immediately.

TABBOULEH

SERVES 4

INGREDIENTS

- 1 3/4 (425 mL) cooked bulgur
  (see cooking method, p. 222)
- 2 medium ripe tomatoes, deseeded and finely chopped
- 1 green onion, thinly sliced
- 2 cloves garlic, peeled and crushed
- 2 cups (500 mL) finely chopped fresh parsley
- 3 Tbsp (45 mL) freshly squeezed lemon juice
- 2 Tbsp (30 mL) extra-virgin olive oil
- Salt and pepper to taste

- In a salad bowl, combine all ingredients and mix thoroughly. Refrigerate 30 minutes before serving.

THREE-CHEESE MACARONI

SERVES 4

INGREDIENTS

- 2 cups (500 mL) macaroni made with soya flour
- 1 Tbsp (15 mL) olive oil
- 1 1/2 cups (625 mL) crushed tomatoes
- 1 clove garlic, peeled and crushed
- 2 Tbsp (30 mL) finely chopped fresh parsley
- Salt and pepper to taste
- 1/2 cup (125 mL) grated sharp cheddar cheese
- 1/2 cup (125 mL) grated part-skimmed mozzarella cheese
- 1/4 cup (50 mL) freshly grated Parmesan cheese

- Preheat oven to 350°F (180°C).

- Cook macaroni in boiling salted water 10 minutes, and drain.
  Place in an ovenproof dish, add olive oil, tomatoes, garlic
  and parsley. Season with salt and pepper, and mix well.

- Cover with the cheeses, and bake about 30 minutes.

VEGETARIAN CHILI

SERVES 4

INGREDIENTS

- 1 Tbsp (15 mL) olive oil
- 2 medium onions, finely chopped
- 1 celery stick, finely sliced
- 3 cloves garlic, peeled and crushed
- 1 small eggplant, peeled and diced
- 1 zucchini, diced
- 5 cups (1.25 L) crushed tomatoes
- 1-2 Tbsp (15-30 mL) chili powder
- 1 Tbsp (15 mL) cumin powder
- 1 Tbsp (15 mL) dried oregano
- 1 Tbsp (15 mL) dried basil
- 1/2 tsp (2 mL) cayenne pepper
- 1 yellow pepper, diced
- 1 green pepper, diced
- 1 cup (250 mL) cooked red kidney beans
  (see cooking method, p. 220)
- 1 cup (250 mL) cooked black beans
  (see cooking method, p. 220)
- Salt to taste

- In a large saucepan, heat olive oil, add onions, celery and garlic, and cook over low heat 5 minutes.

- Add eggplant, cover, and cook 10 minutes more, stirring occasionally.

- Add zucchini, tomatoes and seasonings (except salt), mix well, partially cover and simmer 30 minutes, stirring occasionally.

- Stir in peppers and beans, add salt to taste, partially cover and continue cooking about 20 minutes more.

WILD RICE SALAD

INGREDIENTS

- 3 cups (750 mL) cooked wild rice
  (see cooking method, p. 222)
- 1/4 cup (50 mL) thinly sliced raw almonds
- 1/4 red or yellow pepper, diced
- 1/4 green pepper, diced
- 1/2 stalk celery, diced
- 1 Tbsp (30 mL) finely chopped red onion
- Balsamic vinaigrette or bruschetta
  (see recipes, pp. 59 and 68)

- In a salad bowl, mix together all ingredients. Season with balsamic vinaigrette or bruschetta, or both. Toss thoroughly. Let stand 15 minutes before serving.

DESSERTS

CHOCOLATE CUSTARD

SERVES 3 TO 4

INGREDIENTS

- 3 cups (750 mL) milk
- 4 large eggs
- 3 Tbsp (45 mL) fructose
- 1/4 cup (50 mL) stone-ground wholewheat flour, sifted
- 3 1/2 oz (100 g) unsweetened chocolate, containing at least 70% chocolate liquor or cocoa

- Bring milk to a boil, then remove from heat, and let cool about 10 minutes.

- Meanwhile, in a bowl, beat eggs, gradually adding fructose and flour. Pour in milk, whisking constantly. Transfer to a saucepan and heat over medium heat, stirring constantly, 5 minutes, or until mixture is thick and creamy.

- Break chocolate into pieces. In a double boiler, place chocolate and 1 Tbsp water, and melt over low heat, stirring constantly. Using a whisk, add cream to melted chocolate, raise heat to medium, and cook 1 minute more.

- Serve chilled or at room temperature.

CHOCOLATE MOUSSE

SERVES 4 TO 6

INGREDIENTS

- 3 1/2 oz (100 g) unsweetened chocolate, containing at least 70% chocolate liquor or cocoa
- 3 large egg yolks
- 2-3 Tbsp (30-45 mL) fructose
- 5 large egg whites
- 3/4 cup (175 mL) 35% m.f. cream

- Break chocolate into pieces. In a double boiler, over low heat, place chocolate pieces and 1 Tbsp water, and melt, stirring with a spatula.

- In a mixing bowl, beat egg yolks and half the fructose until frothy. Gradually add melted chocolate, beating continuously, and set aside.

- In a separate bowl, beat egg whites until stiff peaks have formed, and set aside.

- In a third bowl, beat cream with rest of fructose until cream is thick.

- With a spatula, gently fold cream, then egg whites, into chocolate mixture. Transfer to 4 or 5 individual serving bowls and refrigerate 5 hours before serving.

COCONUT CUSTARD
WITH BERRIES

SERVES 4

INGREDIENTS

- 2 large whole eggs
- 4 large egg yolks
- 1/4 cup (50 mL) fructose
- 1/4 tsp (1 mL) salt
- 1/4 tsp (1 mL) pure vanilla extract
- 2 cups (500 mL) milk
- 3 Tbsp (45 mL) unsweetened grated coconut
- 3 Tbsp (45 mL) chopped walnuts (optional)
- Berries (raspberries, strawberries, blackberries)

- Preheat oven to 300°F (150°C).

- In a mixing bowl, beat whole eggs, egg yolks, fructose, salt and vanilla extract. In a saucepan, bring milk to barely simmering, and beat in egg mixture.

- Pour into 6 individual ramekins; place into a shallow pan of water, and bake 1 hour.

- Unmould each ramekin onto a plate, sprinkle coconut and nuts over, and serve with whole berries, or a purée of berries.

COCONUT MOUNDS

SERVES 4

INGREDIENTS

- 3 1/2 oz (100 g) unsweetened chocolate, containing at least 70% chocolate liquor or cocoa
- 1/4 cup (50 mL) chopped raw nuts
- 1/4 cup (50 mL grated unsweetened coconut

- Break chocolate into pieces. In a double-boiler, over low heat, melt chocolate with 1 Tbsp water. Remove from heat. Stir in nuts and coconut.

- Spoon mixture onto wax sheet or nonstick pan, and refrigerate 1 hour.

CRÈME BRÛLÉE

SERVES 3 TO 4

INGREDIENTS

- 1 fresh vanilla bean
- 1 cup (250 mL) 15% m.f. heavy cream
- 1 cup (250 mL) milk
- 3 large egg yolks
- 3 Tbsp (45 mL) fructose

- Split vanilla bean and scrape out the tiny black seeds with a spoon.

- In a saucepan, place cream, milk, vanilla bean and seeds, and bring to boil. Remove from heat, and let stand 15 minutes. Remove vanilla bean.

- Preheat oven to 300°F (150°C).

- In a bowl, beat egg yolks with fructose until blended and fluffy. Add cream mixture, and whisk. Pour into 4 individual ramekins, place in a shallow pan of water and bake 35 to 45 minutes, or until cream starts to thicken. Refrigerate at least 2 hours.

- Before serving, sprinkle each portion with a pinch of fructose, and broil 1 to 2 minutes until tops are brown and caramelized.

ENGLISH CUSTARD

SERVES 4

INGREDIENTS

- 4 large egg yolks
- 2 Tbsp (30 mL) fructose
- 1/4 tsp (1 mL) pure vanilla extract
- 3/4 cup (175 mL) milk

- In a mixing bowl, beat egg yolks, fructose and vanilla extract about 2 minutes.

- Add milk, and beat 2 minutes more, or until mixture is frothy.

- Place the bowl in a pan of hot water, and whisk mixture continuously over medium heat 5 to 6 minutes, or until custard thickens.

- Remove from heat, and whisk well to cool mixture. Cover with plastic wrap and refrigerate about 1 hour. Serve with berries or use as filling for a tart.

- *Variation:* For a different flavour, add 1 Tbsp. unsweetened shredded coconut to the mixture while bowl is in pan of hot water (step 3).

FROZEN BERRY SOUFFLÉ

SERVES 4

INGREDIENTS

- 2 cups (500 mL) fresh berries (raspberries, strawberries, blackberries); if using frozen berries, defrost
- 1/4 cup (50 mL) fructose
- 3 large egg yolks
- 3/4 cup (175 mL) 35% m.f. cream, whipped
- 1/2 cup (125 mL) 5% m.f. ricotta cheese
- Fresh mint leaves and berries for garnish

- Tie a paper collar (wax paper or baking parchment) secured with string under the rim of each of 4 individual ramekins; paper should be 1 inch (2.5 cm) taller than ramekins.

- In a food processor or blender, purée berries while adding fructose. Transfer to a large bowl and set aside.

- In a separate bowl, beat egg yolks until frothy.

- With a spatula, gently fold egg yolks, whipped cream and ricotta into puréed berries. Spoon mixture into ramekins and freeze 3 hours.

- Remove paper, and garnish with mint leaves and berries before serving.

FROZEN CHOCOLATE YOGURT

SERVES 4

INGREDIENTS

- 3 1/2 oz (100 g) unsweetened chocolate, containing at least 70% chocolate liquor or cocoa
- 1 1/2 cup (375 mL) plain yogurt
- 1/4 cup (50 mL) fructose
- 1 large egg white

- Break chocolate into pieces, and melt in a double boiler (or bain-marie) with 1 Tbsp water, stirring with a spatula.

- In a bowl, beat yogurt with fructose 1 minute. Gradually add melted chocolate, beating constantly, until well blended. Spread mixture in a large dish and freeze at least 8 hours.

- Using a knife, cut frozen mixture into pieces. Transfer to food processor and process to just until pieces are smaller. Add egg white, and process until mixture is creamy.

- Serve immediately.

- *Variation:* Add 2 to 3 Tbsp ground almonds or hazelnuts to yogurt-chocolate mixture before freezing.

FRUIT SALAD WITH CHEESE MOUSSE

SERVES 4

INGREDIENTS

- 1/3 lb (150 g) light Philadelphia cream cheese (or similar brand)
- 3 Tbsp (45 mL) fructose
- 1/4 tsp (1 mL) natural vanilla extract
- 2 large egg whites
- 1 1/2 cups (375 mL) fresh strawberries, quartered
- 1 cup (250 mL) fresh raspberries
- 2 kiwi fruit, peeled and cut into small pieces

- In a bowl, beat cream cheese with 1 Tbsp fructose and the vanilla extract. Set aside.

- In another bowl, beat egg whites until soft peaks are formed. Gradually add rest of fructose, and beat until egg whites are shiny and peaks are stiff.

- With a spatula, gently fold egg whites into cream cheese until well blended. Gently fold in fruit, and refrigerate 1 hour before serving.

GLAZED APPLE TART

SERVES 4 TO 6

INGREDIENTS

- 4 apples, peeled and cored
- 2/3 cup (175 mL) unsweetened apple sauce
- 1/2 cup (125 mL) unsweetened apricot jam
- 1 tsp (5 mL) cinnamon
- 1/4 cup fructose

TART CRUST

- 2 large egg whites
- 1 Tbsp (15 mL) fructose
- 3/4 cup (175 mL) ground almonds
- 1/2 cup (125 mL) ground hazelnuts

- *To make the crust:* Beat egg whites until soft peaks form. Gradually add fructose until peaks are stiff and shiny. With a spatula, gently fold in ground almonds and hazelnuts until well blended.

- Preheat oven to 325°F (160°C).

- Spread crust mixture in a nonstick pie dish, and bake 8 to 10 minutes. Let cool.

- Meanwhile, cut apples in two, then slice into thin half-moon slices.

- Spread apple sauce evenly on crust, cover with apple slices, arranging them in concentric circles. Sprinkle with fructose and cinnamon. Bake in 400°F (200°C) oven 25 minutes.

- In a saucepan, over low heat, heat apricot jam with 1 Tbsp (15 mL) water 1 to 2 minutes. Brush mixture over tart, and bake 5 minutes or until apples are tender when tested with the tip of a knife.

LEMON SORBET

SERVES 4

INGREDIENTS

- 4 cups (1 L) water
- 1 cup (250 mL) fructose
- Zest of 2 medium fresh lemons
- Juice of 4 medium fresh lemons
- 1 large egg white

- In a saucepan, combine water and fructose, and bring to boil. Add zest, and boil 5 minutes. Let cool about 20 minutes.

- Add lemon juice, stir, and strain through a fine-mesh sieve into a plastic container with a tight lid. Store in freezer 8 hours, or until mixture is solid.

- In a small bowl, beat egg white until fluffy. Set aside.

- With a knife, cut frozen lemon mixture into large pieces. Place in a blender or food processor and process until pieces are tiny. Add egg white, and process until creamy. Return to freezer 1 to 3 hours before serving.

- *Variation:* To make an orange sorbet, replace lemon zest with zest of 1 1/2 oranges, and lemon juice with juice of 3 oranges.

MANGO SWEET

SERVES 4 TO 6

INGREDIENTS

- 3 medium mangos, peeled, pit removed and cut into pieces
- 1/2 lb (225 g) soft tofu
- 1 cup (250 mL) 5% m.f. ricotta cheese
- 1-2 Tbsp (15-30 mL) fructose
- 1/4 tsp (1 mL) pure vanilla extract

- In a food processor or blender, process all ingredients until smooth and creamy. Refrigerate at least 1 hour before serving.

PEARS POACHED IN WINE

SERVES 4

INGREDIENTS

- 4 ripe, firm pears
- 1 1/2 cups (375 mL) red wine
- 1/4 cup (50 mL) fructose
- 2 Tbsp (30 mL) freshly squeezed lime juice

- Peel pears, cut in half lengthwise, and remove core.

- In a saucepan, bring wine, fructose and lime juice to boil, stirring constantly to dissolve fructose. Add pears, partially cover, and simmer 15 minutes, or until pears are tender.

- Serve chilled or at room temperature.

RASPBERRY & ALMOND DELIGHT

SERVES 4

INGREDIENTS

- 2 medium egg whites
- 3 Tbsp (45 mL) fructose
- 1/2 tsp (2 mL) pure almond extract
- 1 1/2 cups (375 mL) raspberries, fresh or frozen and defrosted
- 1 1/2 cups (375 mL) 5% m.f. ricotta cheese
- 2 Tbsp (30 mL) sliced almonds

- In a mixing bowl, beat egg whites until soft peaks form. Add fructose and almond extract and continue beating until peaks are firm.

- In a blender or food processor, purée raspberries. Using a spatula, combine purée and ricotta, then gently fold in egg whites, until well blended.

- Transfer to 4 individual serving bowls, and garnish with almond slices.

RASPBERRY BAVARIAN CREAM

SERVES 8

INGREDIENTS

- 2 cups (500 mL) raspberries, fresh or frozen and defrosted
- 2 Tbsp (30 mL) unsweetened gelatin powder
- 1/2 cup (125 mL) cold water
- 1/4 cup (50 mL) boiling water
- 1/3 cup (75 mL) fructose
- 1 Tbsp (15 mL) freshly squeezed lime juice
- 1 tsp (5 mL) pure vanilla extract
- 2 large egg whites
- 1 cup (250 mL) 35% m.f. cream, whipped
- Fresh mint leaves and whole raspberries for garnish

- In a food processor or blender, purée raspberries, and set aside.

- In a bowl, sprinkle gelatin over cold water and let stand 5 minutes. Add boiling water, stirring until gelatin is dissolved. Add raspberry purée, half the fructose, lime juice and vanilla extract. Stir well, and refrigerate, stirring occasionally, about 20 minutes or until mixture has thickened.

- In a separate bowl, beat egg whites, add remaining fructose and continue beating until soft peaks have formed. Gently fold egg whites into raspberry mixture, then fold in cream.

- Pour into individual ramekins, and refrigerate at least 3 hours, until set.

- Unmould bavarian creams onto a serving dish, and garnish with mint leaves and raspberries.

RASPBERRY CHEESECAKE

SERVES 8

INGREDIENTS

- 8 oz (250 g) light Philadelphia cream cheese (or similar brand)
- 1 cup (250 mL) 5% m.f. ricotta cheese
- 1/2 cup (125 mg) fructose
- 1/2 tsp (2 mL) pure vanilla extract
- 1 large egg
- 2 cups (500 mL) raspberries, fresh or frozen and defrosted

TART CRUST

- 2 large egg whites
- 1 Tbsp (15 mL) fructose
- 3/4 cup (175 mL) ground almonds
- 1/2 cup (125 mL) ground hazelnuts

- *To make the crust:* Beat egg whites until soft peaks form. Gradually add fructose until peaks are stiff and glossy. With a spatula, gently fold in ground almonds and hazelnuts until well blended.

- Preheat oven to 325°F (160°C).

- Spread crust mixture in a nonstick pie dish, and bake 5 minutes. Reserve.

- In a bowl, beat cheeses with half the fructose and vanilla. Add egg and beat well. Pour into pie dish, and bake at 350°F (180°C) 35 minutes, or until centre is almost done. Let cool about 20 minutes.

- Meanwhile, in a small saucepan, over low heat, cool raspberries and rest of fructose 10 minutes, stirring occasionally.

- Spread over the tart, and refrigerate 3 hours before serving.

RASPBERRY SNOW

SERVES 4

INGREDIENTS

- 2 cups (500 mL) raspberries, fresh or frozen and thawed
- 1/4 cup (50 mL) fructose
- 1 cup (250 mL) plain yogurt
- 1/4 cup (50 mL) 5% m.f. sour cream
- 1/4 tsp (1 mL) freshly grated orange zest
- 1/4 tsp (1 mL) pure vanilla extract
- Fresh mint leaves for garnish

- In a mixing bowl, combine raspberries and fructose. Let stand 20 minutes, stirring occasionally.

- In another bowl, combine yogurt, sour cream, orange zest and vanilla extract.

- Divide 1/3 of raspberry mixture into 4 sorbet glasses; to each add 2 Tbsp yogurt mixture. Repeat procedure with a layer of raspberry mixture, and a layer of yogurt mixture.

- Top with remaining raspberry mixture, and finish with 1 Tbsp of yogurt mixture. Garnish with mint leaves and serve.

STRAWBERRY COULIS

MAKES 1 1/4 CUP (300 ML)

INGREDIENTS

- 2 cups (500 mL) strawberries, fresh or frozen and defrosted
- 1-2 Tbsp (15-30 mL) fructose
- 1 tsp (5 mL) freshly squeezed lime juice

- In a blender or food processor, purée strawberries. Transfer purée to a small saucepan, add fructose and lime juice, and cook over low heat 10 minutes, stirring occasionally.

- Serve hot or at room temperature.

- *Variation:* Use raspberries or kiwi fruit instead of strawberries.

- *Serving tip:* Delicious served with custard or crème caramel.

STRAWBERRY MOUSSE

SERVES 4

INGREDIENTS

- 1 Tbsp (15 mL) unsweetened gelatin powder
- 1/4 cup (50 mL) water or juice of defrosted strawberries
- 1 cup (250 mL) strawberries, fresh or frozen and defrosted
- 1/2 cup (125 mL) plain yogurt
- 2 large egg whites
- 1/4 cup (50 mL) fructose

- In a small pan, place water or juice and sprinkle gelatin over. Let sit 5 minutes, then over low heat, dissolve and stir well.

- In a bowl, mix strawberries, yogurt and gelatin. Refrigerate until mixture begins to set, that is, until it has the consistency of raw egg whites.

- In a separate bowl, beat egg whites until soft peaks form. Gradually add fructose and continue beating until peaks are stiff and shiny.

- Lightly beat about 1/4 of the egg whites into the strawberry mixture, then blend in rest of the egg whites. Pour into 4 individual goblets and refrigerate 1 hour. To serve, garnish with fresh strawberries.

HOW TO COOK LEGUMES

PREPARATION

1. Clean out debris and rinse legumes of your choice (chickpeas, kidney or other type of bean or pea).

2. In a large bowl, soak the legumes in 3 cups of cold water for 10 or more hours, depending on the kind of legume (see chart on p. 221). *Tip:* After soaking, you can freeze a portion to cut the preparation time of your next legume dish.

3. Drain water from legumes and rinse. Place legumes in pot. Fill pot with required amount of cold water for your particular type of legume (see chart on p. 221). Bring the water to a boil, then let simmer for required time (see chart on p. 221) until legumes become tender.

4. To reduce the amount of cooking time, add a 2-inch (5 cm) strip of kombu seaweed in the pot.

5. To decrease flatulence caused by the digestion of legumes, change the cooking water once or twice during cooking time.

6. Adding seasonings such as garlic, onions or savory also help digestion.

LEGUME COOKING CHART

Legumes (for 1 cup/250 mL)	Soaking Time	Cold Water (for cooking)	Cooking Time	Servings
Aduki Beans	10 to 12 hours	2 cups (500 mL)	1 1/2 hours	2 cups (500 mL)
Black-eyed Peas	10 to 12 hours	3 cups (750 mL)	1 hour	3 cups (750 mL)
Black Beans	10 to 12 hours	3 cups (750 mL)	1 to 1 1/2 hours	3 cups (750 mL)
Chickpeas	10 to 12 hours	4 cups (1 L)	1 to 1 1/2 hours	3 cups (750 mL)
Dried Whole Peas	10 to 12 hours	4 cups (1 L)	1 hour	3 cups (750 mL)
Kidney or Red Beans	10 to 12 hours	3 cups (750 mL)	1 to 1 1/2 hours	2 cups (500 mL)
Lentils (Brown)	——	3 cups (750 mL)	45 minutes	2 cups (500 mL)
Lentils (Green)	——	3 cups (750 mL)	30 minutes	2 cups (500 mL)
Lentils (Red)	——	3 cups (750 mL)	30 minutes	2 1/2 cups (625 mL)
Mungo Beans	10 to 12 hours	3 cups (750 mL)	1 to 1 1/2 hours	2 cups (500 mL)
Navy Beans	10 to 12 hours	3 cups (750 mL)	1 hour	3 cups (750 mL)
Pinto Beans	10 to 12 hours	3 cups (750 mL)	1 to 1 1/2 hours	2 cups (500 mL)
Soya Beans	24 hours	4 cups (1 L)	3 to 4 hours	2 cups (500 mL)
Split Peas	——	3 cups (750 mL)	30 to 45 minutes	2 1/2 cups (625 mL)

HOW TO COOK GRAINS

PREPARATION

1. Rinse grains such as rice or barley several times under warm water. Soak if necessary.

2. Boil required amount of water, add the grain of your choice and cover. Reduce heat and cook according to the chart below.

3. Once the cooking is completed, let stand for 5 minutes in covered pot.

GRAIN COOKING CHART

Grains (for 1 cup/250 mL)	Soaking Time	Water (for cooking)	Cooking Time	Servings
Barley	3 to 4 hours	2 cups (500 mL)	45 to 60 minutes	3 cups (750 mL)
Brown Rice	——	2 cups (500 mL)	40 minutes	4 cups (1 L)
Buckwheat	——	2 cups (500 mL)	15 to 20 minutes	3 to 4 cups (750 mL to 1 L)
Bulgur (Cracked Wheat)	——	2 cups (500 mL)	15 to 20 minutes	3 cups (750 mL)
Millet	——	2 cups (500 mL)	20 to 25 minutes	4 cups (1 L)
Quinoa	——	2 cups (500 mL)	12 to 15 minutes	3 cups (750 mL)
Whole Oats	——	2 cups (500 mL)	15 to 20 minutes	2 cups (500 mL)
Wild Rice	——	2 1/2 cups (625 mL)	40 minutes	4 cups (1 L)

A GUIDE TO FINE HERBS
& SPICES

Fresh or dried herbs and spices can be used in a variety of dishes and with a variety of foods. The following will help you find the appropriate herb or spice to flavor your dish.

Anise	Pork, duck, stewed fruit, breads, cakes, cookies
Basil	Fish, seafood, fowl, eggs, lamb, pork, veal, rabbit, cheeses, vegetables, noodles, tomato bases, sauces
Bay Leaves	Sauces, soups, consommés, stews, meat, fowl, fish, vegetables, legumes
Capers	Mayonnaise, mustard, meat, fowl, fish, hors d'oeuvres, rice, sauces
Caraway Seeds	Brochettes, fish, seafood, cheese, lentils, rice, salads, vegetables, fruit
Celery Seed	Vinaigrettes, tomato juice, fish, seafood, legumes
Chervil	Soups, salads, vinaigrettes, stews, veal, fish, omelettes, sauces
Chili Peppers	Vinaigrettes, sauces, meat, stews, soups, seafood, olives
Chives	Vinaigrettes, salads, vegetables, soups, fish, meat, omelettes
Cinnamon	Cakes, cookies, pancakes, bread, stewed fruit, apples, peaches, pears, yogurts, stews, meats, chicken, turkey, tomato sauce
Cloves	Stews, beef, hams, apples, cakes, cookies, tomato sauce
Coriander	Cheese, omelettes, rice, cookies, cakes, breads

Cumin	Sausages, lamb, cheese, eggs, legumes, rice, tomatoes
Curry	Meat, fowl, vegetables, rice
Dill	Vinaigrettes, pickles, celery root, fish
Garlic	Vinaigrettes, vegetables, stews, meat, fish, fowl, soups, olives, pates, noodles
Ginger	Meat, fowl, fish, rice, sauces, vegetables, fruit, cookies
Herbes de Provence	(Marjoram, Oregano and Thyme) Tomato bases, vinaigrettes, sauces, vegetables, eggs, fish, seafood, fowl, meat
Marjoram	Tomato bases, vinaigrettes, sauces, soups, consommés, stews, meat, fish, legumes, vegetables
Mint	Vinaigrettes, mayonnaise, sour cream, meat, game, fish, sauces, vegetables
Mustard	Vinaigrettes, mayonnaise, pork, fowl, sausages, fish, eggs
Nutmeg	Cakes, stewed fruit, cream, fruit, eggs, cheese, sauces, snails
Onion Powder	Meat, fowl, fish, salads, vegetables
Oregano	Tomato bases, vinaigrettes, sauces, soups, consommés, stews, meat, fish, legumes, vegetables
Paprika	Stews, fowl, eggs, vegetables
Parsley	Soups, stews, meat, fowl, fish, vegetables
Pepper	Meat, fowl, fish, sauces, cheese, noodles, vegetables, vinaigrettes
Poppy Seed	Breads, bagels, cakes, cheese, vegetables
Rosemary	Soups, meat, game, fowl, fish, salad
Saffron	Soups, rice, cheese, eggs, stews, meat, fowl, fish
Sage	Stews, meat, fish, omelettes, cheese, soups, vegetables

Savory	Soups, stews, meat, games, fish, eggs, sauces, salads, vegetables, vinaigrettes, legumes
Tarragon	Eggs, fish, fowl, soups, salads, tomatoes, sauces
Thyme	Soups, stews, game, meat, fish, fowl, eggs, sauces, tomato sauce, legumes, vegetables
Watercress	Salads, fish, seafood

N.B.: If you would rather use a fresh herb than a dried one, triple the suggested amount in any given recipe.

LEXICON

Bain-marie	Also known as a double boiler. To place a container in a pot halfway filled with hot water in order to melt its contents slowly without burning. Example: chocolate pieces.
Beat	To use an electric beater or whisk to render foods such as egg whites stiff and vinaigrettes frothy.
Bed	To lay down a cut of meat or other item on top of a garnish, such as a bed of lettuce or rice.
Blanket	To cover a dish with a sauce.
Brochette	Skewered meat and/or vegetables for broiling.
Brown	To fry meat or vegetables in a saucepan coated with oil or other fat until it becomes brown.
Brush	To coat meat, vegetables or other foods with a liquid such as a marinade.
Chop	To cut up into little pieces.
Defat	To remove the layer of fat that forms on a liquid when it is cooled. Also to remove excess fat from a piece of meat.
Deglaze	To dissolve the caramelized particles of meat remaining in a pan after roasting or sautéing by adding a liquid and heating.
Deseed	To remove seeds from a fruit or vegetable.
Dice	To cut pieces of food into small cubes.
Escalope	A fine slice of veal or turkey.
Fold	To gently incorporate a food ingredient into a mixture by slow, deliberate turns.
Golden	To place food in the oven to give it a golden hue.
Gratin	A brown crust on foods formed by melted cheese.
Grill	To place on a flat, hot surface without benefit of oil, such as a griddle, skillet or barbecue grill.

Marinate	To soak a food in a preparation to imbue it with a certain flavour and/or render it tender.
Papillote	To wrap a food in aluminum foil before cooking.
Poach	To cook a food in a simmering liquid, such as salmon or eggs.
Powder	To spread by gently shaking a substance such as sugar or cinnamon over a food.
Sauté	Literally to jump, sauté means to quickly fry by stirring constantly in very little oil over extreme heat.
Sear	To seal in the juices of a meat over high heat.
Season	To add spices and herbs to food to give it flavour.
Shell	To take off the outer casing of seafood. To remove peas from a pod.
Simmer	To bring water right up to the boiling point.
Slice	To cut in fine pieces.
Soak	To clean and blanch meat by placing it in cold water.
Stir	To move liquids in soups or stews in a circular motion in a pot or pan in order to keep them from burning.
Strain	To filter foods by using a sieve or colander.
Whip	To beat a substance at high speeds to infuse it with air, thereby increasing its volume. Examples: whipped cream or egg whites into meringue.

Québec, Canada
1999